Music in Churches

Nourishing Your Congregation's Musical Life

Linda J. Clark

AN ALBAN INSTITUTE PUBLICATION

The Publications Program of The Alban Institute is assisted by a grant from Trinity Church, New York City.

Library of Congress #94-78334
ISBN 1-56699-134-X

CONTENTS

Preliminary Remarks about the Book

This book is an examination of a very ordinary phenomenon—church music. It relies, in large measure, on the voices of people who sing and play music in church. In churches all over the land, music gives voice to faith. These voices of faith were collected over a four year period in a study entitled the Music in Churches Project, undertaken by myself and others under the auspices of Boston University School of Theology and supported through a series of grants from the Lilly Endowment of Indianapolis. My intention in writing this book is to provide an understanding of the practice of church music and set guidelines for the use of music in worship, based on the findings of the project. In the book, I will discuss important normative issues provoked by the material of the research project. I will provide not only "tips" and "advice" but also the means by which to evaluate, accept, or discard them—practical information as well as underlying presuppositions.

The material in the book is derived from studies of local congregations. I went into local churches to find out how ordinary people make connections between music and their faith. My work is based on the assumption that since a congregation is the locale of the vocation, it has to be the locale of research about it. This is not a moral statement but a philosophical one, based on an epistemology of practice. Not that an "expert" simply records the religious practices she or he finds in a congregation without recourse to theories and historical precedents; but without such grounding, the material of any book, in my view, lacks vital substance and risks being irrelevant.

Moreover, the book's grounding in the religious practices of music making and of the praise of God in local congregations helps to widen the scope of the discussion to include the congregations doing the music making as well as *all* professionals responsible for leadership on Sunday morning, pastors and musicians alike. Because the data of the project include as much information about faith as they do about music, the book also will provide information about the spiritual formation of congregations. It is of value to anyone interested in congregations and their life of faith, as well as practicing church musicians, pastors, and lay leaders.

An Initial Look at the Issues

The story found between the covers of this book is very complex and often contradictory. Themes vary as each community varies, and sometimes within each of these communities there are strong contradictions. Although on the surface the practice of making music in church seems rather straightforward and unremarkable, it is not.

As an introduction to the issues that come to bear on the practice of church music, let us take an initial look at one of the congregations in the study. In this church, the music program was well established: The organist/choir master was a member of a local college faculty; there was a good senior choir and a good organ in the sanctuary. Yet, at the time of the project, some complaints were being fielded by one of the clergy members of the staff.

In an interview with the staff, the following exchange took place. The priest who had been hearing the complaints brought up the subject of hymn singing:

> I feel good about the hymns going with the lessons, but easy to sing? I think that's the one area in which I hear complaints. They're often hymns that the choir can sing well, but I've heard several complaints from people who say they couldn't sing the harmony, or that it was one they just couldn't sing. It was a difficult tune, or they wished there were some that were more contemporary, and maybe simpler.

The priest was talking about a tension she sensed in this congregation: between standards of excellence shared by the organist/choir master and a large part of the congregation, and the desire, also shared by a large number, for easily accessible hymns for singing. This comment

led to a discussion of their methods of evaluating what they were doing.
The organist/choir master raised the issue of familiarity and its lingering
power.

> Well, I've been in this racket long enough to know that I cer-
> tainly cannot depend upon others. For one thing, in church music,
> you don't get feedback. What feedback you do get from others is
> liable to be special pleading—it's liable to be "I like that!" and what
> that's liable to mean is "It reminds me of an anthem we used to sing
> in St. Swithin's in the Swamp forty years ago." Or when it's nega-
> tive, that's liable to mean, "We never did anything like that at St.
> Swithin's in the Swamp." It's very rarely based upon anything,
> either musical or spiritual, that is appropriate to St. Thomas. . . .
> That probably sounds pretty stuffy—I mean it strikes me that what
> I'm really saying is that I'll decide whether it's good or bad, thank
> you very much.

A member of the clergy countered by describing the importance of
familiarity to the worship life of a congregation.

> Well, I don't know. Your comment about verbal response and
> what that frequently will mean—whether it's positive or negative—
> brings to mind a workshop that I went to. The leader was talking
> about ritual, and, he said, the purpose of ritual is to recreate, to bring
> back a moment, if you will, or a piety. What I'm saying is that may-
> be it *does* remind us of St. Swithin's in the Swamp, but maybe that
> was a very important time of life for them. There's power in that.

Another staff member made a comment that broadened the discussion. He described a situation where familiarity was a barrier to worship
and then talked about making judgments about their work based both on
the life of the congregation and the truths of the tradition.

> What I heard Sam saying was not so much that it's bad to be
> back at St.—you know, to have those echoes—but that you can't
> judge the quality of what you do by the response of people who,
> because they didn't do that kind [of thing at] St. Swithin's, don't
> know how to respond to the music *here*. . . .
> Part of our job is to do the best we can in ways that give our

best understandings of ourselves and of the nature of the liturgy and of the congregation—to build over time a liturgy that embodies both the truth of what we're doing and the life of the congregation. And in the end, the indicators—like hymn singing—are not what people say about what we do, it's that sense of a relationship that an actor has with an audience. It has nothing to do with applause. It's a voice that comes back at you out of the congregation. It's that sense of concentration between the chancel and the nave . . . .

Finally the rector made a statement that ended the conversation.

I think all of us are really members of this congregation, and that the communication has always been pretty rapid and pretty good. Even without polls. I definitely do not get the sense of any-one of the four of us going off in a cocked hat in some direction that is not appropriate, or not conceivably sanctioned.

Yet the researchers in the project uncovered quite a lot of contro-versy about the music program that seemed not to have surfaced, at least in this conversation about their work. The comments about the difficulty of the hymns were indicators of other problems.
One woman interviewed was very annoyed about the postlude:

[People] go up [into the chancel] and usually Sam *blasts* on the organ at the very end of the service. It is so loud it drives you out of the church. You cannot carry on a conversation, which is too bad, because it's one way of fellowship. And I feel very strongly that the people look at the ones that are not sitting there, listening to the mu-sic, and they're saying, "Oh, aren't they rude! They're talking while the music is going on." My feeling is that the *music is rude.*

Another person voiced a desire to expand the style of the music that was used in the liturgy on Sunday. When asked what he would do if he were church musician for a week, he said:

Well, I think I would do several things. I think that our lack of attention to the gospel type of music is something that I—I'm not sure how, quite how I would do it, but I would try and remedy. And I would try not to do this over Sam's dead body!

He went on to describe worship in another church he attends frequently, when he is visiting his daughter:

> I have the experience of an Episcopal church in upstate New York where there is a nine o'clock service that is based around this kind of music, a very informal gospel-type of Eucharist service, where, for example, for the actual serving of the Eucharist, people form a cross. And they pass a loaf of bread, tear off bread, and pass wine. And sing a very lively kind of music, with a very small choir. And piano rather than an organ, and it's a marvelously uplifting service, and it's very interesting because, from the community, there are a number of older people, including some retired college professors and all, as well as young people and people with families who come to this nine o'clock service.

Central Questions

The controversies in this church are very familiar ones; indeed, few music programs in the project *lacked* controversy. Most everyone would agree that there is some sort of responsibility of the staff for the congregation, but what kind? Surely the staff are not there simply to win popularity contests.

There are no simple solutions to the issues that were raised here because the conflicts about music in this church were really conflicts about worship and the community who gathered to do it. The interrelationship between music and faith is evident in the interchange in the staff and in the interviews. Everyone moved from the music to speak of what the music was doing or should be doing.

These are the basic questions that I see this staff trying to address. They are also the central questions that I will address in this book:

1. *How is the music program functioning in the worship life of this congregation; i.e., the relationship between music and the faith life of the congregation?*

2. *What does it serve? To whom are the staff accountable in planning music; i.e., the role of leadership?*

3. *Are the methods by which the music program functions actually achieving what the staff thinks should be happening; i.e., the type and efficiency of the work being done?*

In this instance, as in most, the staff needed more information from the congregation—and more reliable and less anecdotal information. But the search for information does not end with polling the congregation. The responsibility of the staff extends to the tradition of the church, the history of the particular congregation, and the biblical heritage which gives it its life and its purpose. One of the staff members alluded to this broader understanding of their responsibility:

> Part of our job is to do the best we can in ways that give our best understandings of ourselves and of the nature of the liturgy and of the congregation—to build over time a liturgy that embodies both the truth of what we're doing and the life of the congregation.

So there is another question to be asked:

4. *Does the music program have integrity within the context of the religious tradition of the congregation; i.e., the norms of evaluation?*

The Music in Churches Project

Many of these questions were in the back of my mind when I attended a meeting of the North American Academy of Liturgy in January of 1986. I was listening to a liturgical scholar describe a project he and others from the University of Notre Dame were working on, one aspect of which addressed liturgical change since Vatican II. In the midst of his speech he made the following observation about music in Catholic churches: "The reason that Catholic congregations do not sing at Mass is not that they do not *want* to sing; it's because what they are given to sing *they do not like.*"

"Now, that's interesting!" I thought. If a local church musician finds that his or her congregation is not singing, the solutions would need to be different under each circumstance. How would these musicians get the information they needed so that they didn't try to solve the wrong problem? How would they know that the answer to their questions lay with the congregation and not the hymnal committee of the denomination or the clergy they had to report to? And if they decided that the answer needed to come from the congregation, how would they go about finding out the real feelings and ideas of a group of people who communicate to them in rather sketchy ways such as, "Good anthem, this morning, Sam," or "You're playing the hymns too slow again!"

This man's statement reoriented my scholarly viewpoint a full 180 degrees. Instead of seeking the answers to my questions about music in the church among scholars and in libraries, I decided to develop a systematic way of asking the people in pews and choir lofts what they thought and felt about it. Over the past four years I have collected the ideas and sentiments of hundreds of ordinary Christians. The reader will hear many of their voices in this book.

The project, based in part on the Notre Dame Study of Catholic Parish Life and the Georgetown/Notre Dame Study of the liturgy since Vatican II, is designed to study the relationship between the faith of the people who gather in a particular congregation for worship on Sunday morning and the music that they make there. It is based on the idea that art is an *event* in which the life embodied in an art work and the life of the beholder or performer meet. Music is not a piece of paper with dark spots on it but an experience or, more correctly, an "experiencing." Music as event is about experiencing something—faith, for instance.

The Design Described

Early on in the project, it became clear to me that music programs in churches are not interchangeable and that the study had to be designed in such a way that the culture and faith of the community that gathered were the context out of which the music program was examined and evaluated.

The project consisted of two major bodies of information: one gathered in a questionnaire passed out after worship in twenty-four churches, and another gathered in case studies in eight of those twenty-four. The questionnaire was designed to put the musical lives of a congregation within the context of their faith lives. Thus, not only did it ask questions about music, it also asked about why people come to church, why they worship, and who they are. The case studies consisted of several views of one worship service, gathered through interviews and onsite participant/observer research by a team of sociologists, liturgists, and musicians. In all it was a very complex project because the relationship studied is very complex. I must admit that the actual running of the project among hundreds of people in twenty-four different communities, most of which were more than a 100 miles from Boston University, brought new meaning for me to the phrase, "Fools rush in where angels fear to tread!"

Limitations of the Data

Given the complexity of the subject matter studied in the project, there were some limitations to what the data told us about music, its use in worship, and the views about it among people in churches.

1. The questionnaire was long and difficult to fill out. Thus, it eliminated many people from the sample, probably those not at all interested in worship in their churches, as well as the people who have trouble reading. The selective nature of the sample is reinforced by the fact that it was passed out after worship and not sent out to the people on the parish rolls. Thus the sample was narrowed to those for whom worship is at least a significant aspect of their connection with a church.

2. Those who did fill out the questionnaire were hesitant to complain about their church. This I dubbed the "best foot forward" syndrome. The questionnaire was designed to offset some of that effect but was not totally successful. The interviews and the team visits brought a much more complete picture of the worship in these churches. Thus the case studies were used to interpret the results from the questionnaire and vice versa.

3. In the case studies, there was on occasion a wide discrepancy between what the people in the church said and felt about their community and what the visiting team discovered. At first, when reading through the case study materials, I tended to disregard their views because their exposure to these congregations was so brief. However, the more I read of their reports the more valuable they seemed, and I concluded that an outsider's view, although partial, was often important.

4. Perhaps the most serious limitation to the data of the project comes from the fact that they are based on what people knew they were experiencing in worship rather than on what they did not know, i.e., all that was unconscious, ineffable, precognitive, mysterious in the experience.

Everyone knows that worship is much more than a conscious exercise. The presence in it of an art form as powerful as music attests to the many layers of experience operating on any given Sunday.

Description of the Sample

Of the approximately 1700 questionnaires passed out in 24 United Methodist and Episcopal churches in Massachusetts, Rhode Island, and Connecticut in November and December of 1988, 835 were returned; 388 were from Episcopalians and 447 were from United Methodists. The median age of those responding was 51. About 40% of them had completed college; 65% considered themselves moderate to liberal politically, 35% conservative; 52% had a total family income of $40,000 or less; 67% lived within three miles of their church. The churches themselves were chosen from among a group of 200 whose representatives initially expressed interest in the project. They were chosen to represent as far as possible a balanced range of four categories: denomination, percentage of the budget allocated for music, process of planning for Sunday worship, and social location (rural, town, suburban, and urban).

The twenty-four churches were predominantly white; there was one church from African-American traditions included. Although there were many other ethnic traditions represented within the congregations, the sample was predominantly English in background (47%).

The eight case study churches were chosen from the original twenty-four largely by the way they answered the question about "worship at its best." Each of the choices in the question was represented. Included among them were a charismatic congregation from each denomination and two churches of each denomination from the same town.

Brief Outline of the Book

The book begins with an explanation of the way music functions to give voice to faith. It then explores the data of the project on worship and its two central musical practices: the singing of the congregation and the singing of the choir. Chapters 5, 6, and 7 put forth ideas and methods for the regulation of a good church music program.

The appendices contain study questions and activities for groups in

churches who wish to explore their own answers to the questions raised
in the book and a bibliography for further reading.

There are many things left out of this book. The most glaring one is
a discussion of the instruments that are used in worship, most notably the
organ. The book also lacks the ongoing diatribes against various trends
and events in the church music world. I omit these for several reasons:
first, there was very little of that in the project, and second, I have tried
not to rehearse my own biases. I realize that this much sought-after
objectivity is impossible to attain. Therefore, let me state my biases as
clearly and as straightforwardly as I can. I am a white, middle-class
Episcopalian, working in a United Methodist Seminary. It was my good
fortune, during the 1970s, to share responsibility for worship at the
Chapel at Union Theological Seminary in New York City with Dr. James
A. Forbes, a black Pentecostal Holiness preacher, now the senior pastor
at Riverside Church in New York City. During this time, I was introduced to Pentecostal forms of music and worship, which I grew to love
and appreciate greatly. Still, I am basically an Episcopalian, but my
experience with a worship and singing tradition so different from my
own has generated in me a strong interest in the music of a variety of
religious traditions and curiosity about others.

I am not a purist. I once planned a worship service at Union that
included both a twelve-tone aria by Daniel Pinkham and an African
American spiritual. But I am a stickler for excellence. That is, the music may come from anywhere, but it has to be done to the best of the
resources available to the congregation.

Once, when I was leaving an ordination service in a little church in
New England where one of my students was the organist and choir
director, the preacher, a member of a local theological faculty, turned to
me and said, "Does being a professional musician make all this kind of
music off-putting [meaning, I suppose, the less-than-professional hymn
singing, the chanting by the congregation, and the choir anthems]?" I
said, "No, it makes it more enjoyable, I think." That was my off-the-cuff
response that day, and the right one, now that I think about it. Being a
musician means having the capacity to respond to shaped sound and its
symbolic power. Becoming a professional musician has intensified that
capacity and made me more open to all forms of music, no matter what
their style, variety, or origin. It has deepened my faith by teaching me to
stand before all of human experience, no matter what its style, its variety,
its origin, with at least a modicum of openness. Thus, I see the role of

the church musician as *both* a performer and a religious educator, whose central task is to seek out ways to give a musical voice to faith.

I wish at this time to thank all of the people who have participated in the Music in Churches Project: the twenty-four churches, their staffs and congregations, and the research teams; the consultants E. Kent Brown, Wade Clark Roof, Horace T. Allen, Jennifer Rike, Lawrence Madden, S.J., James Lopresti, David Leege, Tom Trozzolo, and Ken Kleinman. My particular thanks go to my administrative assistant, Tim Hughes, a wonderful musician and a budding sociologist; and to Elizabeth Bettenhausen, who, through her exhaustive comments on the original reports, deepened my understanding of the relationship between music and faith. Thanks also to the Lilly Endowment for funding the Music in Churches project and to Celia Hahn and The Alban Institute for publishing the research in book form.

CHAPTER 1

Music and Faith

Introduction

The people who work away in the field of church music are not the
heroes or heroines of our society. Most church musicians are paid much
less per year than Larry Bird (of Boston Celtics fame) made per game!
And not much attention is paid to music making in churches among other
professional musicians either, perhaps because of meager resources and
the presence of all those amateurs.

It is a similar sign of neglect when the presuppositions that regu-
late musical activity in worship are not clearly thought out by a local
congregation. All of us are guilty in one way or another of taking this
music making for granted. Too often, the principles governing music for
worship do not emerge from the act of making music in worship. This is
particularly true of the choice of music. Ideas about repertory are often
"imported" from another setting, such as the concert hall or a TV evan-
gelist, or are thinly disguised forms of the personal preferences of the
pastor, the congregation, or the musician.

I first noticed this neglect (I say "noticed" here because I had been
doing it all my life!) in the midst of a struggle about the use of the guitar
in worship at Union Seminary at the end of the 1960s. A faculty member
of the School of Sacred Music, who was also the organist in the chapel,
refused to allow the preacher to include a folk song with guitar accompaniment at the conclusion of his sermon. They had a "battle royal" about
this. On one side, the organist was appalled that his aesthetic standards
were being challenged by a nonmusician; on the other side, the preacher
wanted to use the song because he liked it! In this instance the preacher
won by pulling rank and declaring the "privilege of the pulpit," but then

the musician turned around and "one-upped" him by refusing to play the service! I thought to myself, "How would one resolve such a conflict? Certainly the appeal to taste or personal preference cannot be the sole basis for making judgments about such an important matter." What are guidelines that grow out of the activity itself?

As I studied the results of the project, I came to certain conclusions about the vocation of the church musician. There are three equally important and interrelated principles that form the basis for the regulation of a church music program.

1. All music comes from the life of faith of a congregation. In churches, music works to undergird and make articulate the act of worship, which is one of the primary expressions of the life of faith in a community.

2. There is a discipline that a church musician develops, along with the technical ones demanded of music makers: that is, there are habits of thought and methods of working that insure that there be coherence between what she or he does and the life of faith of the community served.

3. This coherence obtains not only in idea and method but also in practice. In this task, musicians and congregations are interdependent agents, since coherence between music and faith requires not only good leadership but also a congregation willing and able to participate in its musical life.

It is my belief that all decisions in the regulation of music to be used in worship flow from one source: the life of faith of a congregation. Although this is a simple statement, it is not a simple matter. People responsible for music in worship work within the current beliefs and practices of a particular community, but also the Faith to which the community is called—Faith with a capital F—which encompasses more than the faith of the present time.

In this section of the book, I want to address at length the first principle in the list above. Debates about music in church are frequently dominated by aesthetic considerations. I want to broaden the debate and redefine some of its terms to underscore the importance of the purposes for which music is used in church. There music has everything to do with faith and with the corporate life of a group of people; that is, it exists not only for itself but for the purposes of worship and praise by a group of people. Worship is not a concert, and the people who attend church are not an audience. A concert-goer can simply ignore those parts of a concert that are in forms unrecognizable to him or her and focus on those that are. She can also choose to attend another concert. When a member of a congregation comes to church, she or he does not come primarily to hear music, although she might have been drawn there because of the music program. He uses the music as an expression of faith. Moreover, his purposes in attending worship extend beyond the music to other forms of expression in which music is embedded, such as rituals. He also has something at stake in the community that is formed through the act of singing. Once he joins this community, he enters into a relationship with the other people in it. Leaving a community and joining another is not the same as leaving one concert hall and going to another.

Music and Faith

I began the Music in Churches Project with many opinions and precon- ceived notions about music in the church. Many of those ideas have been modified, some discarded. My major hypothesis still stands, how- ever: *At the center of a successful music program is a vital connection between music and the life of faith of a particular congregation.* In wor- ship, music and faith are inextricably linked; the purpose of a church music program is to manifest and make articulate the faith of the people. There are two major facets to this process: expression and formation. Music expresses faith; that is, it is a vehicle through which the faith within a person and a community comes forth. People's favorite hymns and anthems have this function. Music also forms faith. If the hymn or anthem is new and unfamiliar, it confronts a person and a community with a reality with which they must come to terms in order to be faithful. This process of formation can also take place in the midst of a very familiar piece of music—one that the listener or performer hears anew in a very different way. What is entailed in this process?

In order properly to understand the relationship between music and faith, several preliminary ideas need to be put forth for examination. How does art function in a community? What is art, and why does it have the power it usually does in religious communities? I will address these questions using as examples the musical practices of worship.

What Is Art?

The basic premise underlying the work of the project is that art is primarily an *event* rather than a *work* like a painting or a composition. A hymnbook is "incipient" music rather than music itself. When one sings a hymn among people, that event is art. By defining art in these terms one broadens the conventional understanding to include the composer(s), the performer(s), and the relationship they enter into *through* the work one produced and the other has at hand. This relationship is basically one of communication of meaning. To let this meaning emerge, the event itself must be transparent and the participants willing to engage in it.

Here is a lay person talking about one such event in her worship life:

> "I remember the first time that I sang [Malotte's *The Lord's Prayer*] here in this church. I had never done that before, even though I knew the song. It really moved me; I wept; it just overwhelmed me; it really touched me a great deal. I really felt like I was participating in a sacred moment. Everyone holding hands, across the aisles even, gives a sense of Body [of Christ], and family and community. A lot of times when I sing it the things that occur to me are that, as a Body [of believers] being human, we wound each other and hurt each other's feelings, for picayune things, actually, most of the time. And when we talk [sing] about 'Forgive us our trespasses, we forgive those who trespass against us,' that usually zeroes in on me—that we're all singing it together and holding hands together and understanding that's what God means about forgiveness. And then, as the song builds at the end where we sing higher and higher—'For Thine is the glory, and the power'—I associate that with the majesty and power of God—it's awesome, you know. I don't think we could ever fathom that in our normal, mortal being. It sort of lifts you out and gives vision. When we are finished singing, I have a sense of unity, a binding. To stand holding hands afterwards only seems to bind us together further, and there is a desire to pray for people around me, whose hands I may be holding. . . . It's like the power of God that just permeates through your being to others, you know, through the Spirit. When it is over, and we finally drop our hands, it's like disconnecting."

This woman is relating the immediacy of her experience of singing this very familiar prayer. She experiences her own life and the life of the people around her as an integral part of the song. The reality of her own search for forgiveness emerges in the singing: "We wound each other and hurt each other's feelings, for picayune things, actually, most of the time." This realization leads to an experience of forgiveness among the people in her congregation: "We're all singing it together and holding hands together and understanding *that's* what God means about forgiveness." In this event, the meaning that is released through the singing is the singer's meaning, formed and evoked by the composer's structures.

In a famous article, "Art as a Cultural System," the cultural anthropologist Clifford Geertz characterizes art essentially as an event of meaning: "[Art] materialize[s] a way of experiencing; [it] bring[s] a particular cast of mind out into the world of objects, where [people] can look at it. . . ."

He refers to works of art as "primary documents" of the society in which they are found [1976:1478]. To return to our example, this version of the Lord's Prayer "materializes a way of experiencing;" through it, the life of faith—ideas, attitudes, and forms of religious sensibility—is brought out into the world of the local Sunday worship or the evening prayer meeting. There people experience something; their faith becomes lively. This song and all the other music used in worship are primary documents of faith.

Understanding church music in this way helps to explain why such a furor broke out when the recent hymnal committee of the United Methodist Church tried to take "Onward Christian Soldiers" out of their new hymnal. People in the pews were furious because something precious to them was being taken away from them without their say-so. The favorite hymns of a person or a community are not "about" the faith of the people; they *are* their faith!

How does such power attach itself to the black dots on a page? Let's go back to hymns and hymn singing. Hymns and other forms of church music are the Protestant equivalent of the Orthodox icons. What kind of "icon" is a hymn? Obviously we do not hang them on a wall and look at them, like we would those that come from the traditions of Eastern orthodoxy. No, a hymn is a highly complex set of images, both verbal and aural, set in motion through singing. Each word and phrase in that sentence is important, and I will explain each of them in turn.

Hymns as Sets of Images

The images of a particular hymn, both poetic and musical, initially draw
the worshipper into the world of a hymn. "Rock of Ages," "Love
Divine, All Loves Excelling," "A Fountain Filled with Blood," "In the
Garden," the "walking bass" in "For All the Saints," the ascending
melodic line which accompanies the text "Up from the grave he arose,"
the particular harmonic cast to "Let all mortal flesh keep silence,"—these
images evoke a kind of fascination in the worshippers that draws them
into the world of the hymn and holds them there while the meaning is
clarified through experience. Avery Dulles in *Models of the Church*
speaks of the way images "mean" in the religious sphere:

> In the religious sphere, images function as symbols. That
> is to say, they speak to [a person] existentially and find an echo in
> the inarticulate depths of his psyche. Such images communicate
> through their evocative power. They convey a latent meaning that
> is apprehended in a nonconceptual, even a subliminal, way.
> [1974:18]

As Dulles points out, images are evocative and convey *latent* meaning.
They take on the energy of fascination which then "sticks" to the subsequent events to which they are linked by the imagination. Hymn images
accompany the singers throughout their lives and surface in ordinary
places, often without bidding, to reinterpret experience.

Hymns as Images Set in Motion

Singing puts the words of a hymn into motion. Hymns are not static sets
of words on a page but shapes of sound that exist in time, beginning at
one moment, traveling towards a point, and then drawing to a close and
stopping at another moment. This shaping of time heightens the meaning
of texts. The philosopher Susanne Langer explains why. In describing
how music has meaning, she states that "what music can actually reflect
is . . . the morphology of feeling. . . . [It] conveys general forms of
feeling" [1957:238]. In other words, music is an aural image of the shape
of feeling alive. When a congregation sings together, the words of the
hymn come alive to them and mean more than just a statement of fact. In

hymn singing a congregation is pouring out their own hearts. The hymn creates that faith by bringing it into being and therefore is functioning as a symbol of the singers' faith. A hymn does not only *tell of* the faith, it *tells* it, declares it, or bodies it forth.

As a community sings "Were you there when they crucified my Lord?" it journeys back to that hillside so vividly captured in the Christian imagination and relives the faith that that image has carried throughout the ages. Yet what the journey back to that hillside retrieves is *not* the actual experience of the crucifixion itself. If the actual crucifixion were relived, there could be no singing. People could only cry out in response to such horror! No, it is the *meaning* of the crucifixion activated through the images of the hymn that is retrieved. Transformation is possible when the meaning of that event with its joyous outcome in resurrection is attached through the singing of the hymn to present suffering, thereby bringing hope to birth in the soul of the singers. Even standing mute, letting the community take over when one's voice fails, an individual can have suffering transformed through the hope being proclaimed by others.

Here is a woman speaking of her favorite hymn, "O Sacred Head, Sore Wounded:"

> [It] recalls Christ's very human pain with simple, sad reverence. It is quiet and contemplative and reminiscent of my most memorable conversion experience.

Here is her description of her conversion experience:

> [It] was on Good Friday, 1983. I was living in [——] and was fairly heavily involved in a church there. I sang in the adult choir, a commitment I took very seriously. I was praying during the last few minutes of the three-hour service when all at once I was overcome by the presence of Jesus and His suffering, death, and resurrection. I suddenly knew that I was forgiven; that I was loved; that Jesus had been there and was here now for me. I started to sob uncontrollably and wept for some time. That day was a major turning point in my relationship with God.

This woman relates the experience her favorite hymn carries for her. A significant moment in her past is brought into the present, and she reaffirms her faith in its singing.

Hymns function as other religious symbols do. As Avery Dulles remarks: "Symbols transform the horizons of [a person's] life, integrate his perception of reality, alter his scale of values, reorient his loyalties, attachments, and aspirations in a manner far exceeding the powers of conceptual thought" [1974:18]. They are powerful shapers of religious identity.

Musical Forms as Transmitters of History

The music of worship often provokes memories of the past, as that woman's story demonstrates, but it also carries the past in more subtle and profound ways. The theologian Bernard Meland describes how expressive forms, like stories, myths, and hymns, grow out of the *mythos* of a community [1976:113]. He speaks of a level of experience, often subconscious, that precedes and supports what we would recognize as ordinary experience—the sensibilities that declare what is of value, what is cherished, what is intended of a community.

Meland asserts that a community's myths, stories, rituals carry forward the "qualitative dimension of the historical experience" [1987: 118]; they present through symbol and metaphor those aspects of experience that are indirect, emotional, laden with meaning. They *body forth* the tradition. The verb that Meland uses—*body forth*—is very important as a way to describe how *material* and *embodied* this act of transmittal of the history of a people is. "Mythos" incorporates those aspects of the tradition that express and inform the identity of a people—what they value and cherish, what motivates them. It is of the *intentionality* of a community.

From the preceding explanation of art and its power to transform people's lives, it is easy to see why the hymns, chants, and responses of a particular congregation are important to its ongoing faith. A musician coming into a community *joins* a musical tradition, one established through the labor of the musicians and congregations gone before. A newcomer is standing on the shoulders of thousands of invisible singers whose voices saturate the walls of the church. Getting to know the "hymnody of the congregation" is one of the first responsibilities of a new director of music.

The Importance of Aesthetic Qualities

I wish to return to something I said earlier about the nature of the event called "art." I said that it had to be transparent. I use the term *transparency* to describe that quality of music that allows the release of meaning to take place in both the work itself and the "worker" (the singer). Art is an event in which the life embodied in an art work and the life of the beholder or performer meet. In order that any meaning be expressed by a composition, or a painting, or a play, it must work. It must be adequate to the task of evoking or carrying this meaning event. Much music produced is simply flat, opaque, and meaningless. Individual composers may possess little talent for shaping aural images or may lack inspired musical ideas. They may not have developed the skills necessary to create these forms of "sentient life." Or perhaps they possess all the necessary skills but really have nothing interesting to say about the life of faith. They create skeletons which appear to be music but have no vitality—they do not body forth anything.

One choir director confided to the interviewer: "There are a number of things this choir has told people—luckily, they've never said this to me—but they have said to other people, that this [piece of music] simply will not do. The quality of this music is just not high enough for us." These people are making judgments about the transparency of certain music—its capacity to release meaning for them.

Making aesthetic judgments is a necessary part of the task of church musicians, but a highly complex one because of their responsibility to the culture(s) of the congregation. Their own musical taste cannot be the overriding criterion. Yet they cannot simply set musical judgments aside because they are called on to exercise them almost daily. Much more will be said about establishing criteria of judgment about repertory in Chapter 7.

What is Faith?

The answers to the question: "What is faith?" fill libraries. I will simply provide a *brief working definition*—one growing out of the worship life of a congregation. Worship is not the only place where Christians practice their faith. In the hospital room, the board room, the practice room—building housing, studying scores, arguing about the church finances—

people practice their faith. It has both individual and corporate dimensions.

I prefer to think of faith as a verb rather than a noun, thereby emphasizing the experience itself. Faith is an event, not an object—an act rather than a set of precepts. *It is the act of being grasped by God.*

Hymns and other forms of church music are stories or responses to stories growing out of the faith described in Hebrew and Christian Scriptures and the acts of faith of untold millions of people who have witnessed to the power of God in their lives. People responsible for music in worship work within the current faith(s) of a particular community, but also the Faith to which the community is called—Faith with a capital F—which encompasses more than the faith of the present time.

For the church is not just any community, but one with a particular past and a particular future that shape its identity. Paul Hanson, in *The People Called: the Growth of Community in the Bible,* describes the nature of this community:

> The community of faith [portrayed in the Bible] is the people *called.* It is the people *called* forth from diverse sorts of bondage to freedom, *called* to a sense of identity founded on a common bond with the God of righteousness and compassion, and *called* to the twin vocations of worship and participation in the creative, redemptive purpose that unifies all history and is directed to the restoration of the whole creation within a universal order of *shalom* [1987;467].

Starting from the life of faith of a particular congregation does not mean that all music in church is reduced to what is familiar or to what has been used by the congregation in the past to express its faith. It does mean that those responsible for the regulation of a music program must know a great deal about the faith of the community they serve.

Church musicians also function as prophets to their congregations through the presentation of music and texts that challenge the present idolatries. They are harbingers of Faith, with a capital F. The commotion about inclusive language is a signal of one such challenge. The uproar about dissonant hymns and anthems is another. Those who confront the present by singing "a New Song to God" teach new piety and lead a congregation away from the known, which may have become too comfortable.

Conclusion

A successful music program is one that both expresses and forms the faith of the community. It is embedded in the character of each community, its "mythos" and its religious traditions, from within which practical judgments are made. Thus, the first and primary responsibility of a church musician is to learn of the faith of the congregation. Within these parameters, the musicians make music. Such things as attention to performance practice, the musical capacities of the choir, organist and congregation, the quality of the music itself are essential but secondary aspects of the musician's task. The springboard for making choices about music in worship therefore requires a broad understanding of the people who gather on Sunday, their individual and corporate pasts, their ethnicity, their religious traditions, and the purposes for which they gather. Thus people leading music in churches make not only aesthetic decisions but theological and liturgical ones as well.

One of the musicians in the project made the following response to the question, "How should music function in worship?" All the components are there: the nature of the community, the nature of the event, and attention to high standards of music making.

> Well, I think [music in worship] should vary from place to place
> .... I don't think there's a fixed answer to that. I mean I think
> that music can play a lot of different roles in worship. I think that
> there's nothing invalid about a group of people sitting around the
> table in someone's living room and singing a hymn without any
> accompaniment or singing a folk-based hymn or whatever, a
> spiritual kind of hymn. That's just as valid a kind of worship and
> relationship with music to worship as a very formal worship in a
> cathedral-like setting. And I think that the only thing that's es-
> sential to me is that the components of worship be of high quality,
> of as high a quality as those who are responsible for making it can
> produce. . . .

ENDNOTES

Dulles, Avery. *Models of the Church.* Garden City: Doubleday, 1974.

Geertz, Clifford. "Art as a cultural system," *Modern Language Notes* 91 (1976).

Hanson, Paul. *The People Called.* San Francisco: Harper & Row, 1987.

Langer, Susanne K. *Philosophy in a New Key.* Cambridge: Harvard University Press, 1957.

Meland, Bernard. *Fallible Forms and Symbols.* Philadelphia: Fortress Press, 1976.

————— "Myth as a mode of awareness and intelligibility," *American Journal of Theology and Philosophy* 8 (September, 1987).

CHAPTER 2

People Speak of Worship

Introduction

We have been discussing how music expresses and forms faith in order
to understand the central purpose of the church musician. In this chapter,
we will to listen to people in churches talk about worship, the place
where music and faith come together. These two issues were the central
concerns of the Music in Churches project. Because worship is the usual
context for the wedding of these two powerful realities, it took on great
importance in the research. True, music is made in churches in other
contexts—Sunday School, hymn singing at potluck suppers, local Pops
concerts, recitals—but the central act in which music expresses and
forms faith is worship on Sundays.

We turn now to the data of the project to report on its findings.
The material in this chapter is organized into two major sections. The
first is based on answers to a question about worship at its best, taken
mostly from interviews with staff members and lay leaders. The second
is based on interviews with selected lay people conducted immediately
after worship on the Sunday the research team came into their congregation. I have made very few comments about these statements, preferring
to let these people have their say.

A brief cautionary note is appropriate. As in all things religious,
what one thinks consciously about worship at any given point in one's
life may not be its most significant aspect. Moreover, looking at the pictures of congregations at worship painted in thousands of pages of data in
the project, it becomes clear that each church is unique; it has its own
style, each congregation its own ethos. Yet significant patterns have
emerged. This chapter will report these patterns.

People Talk about Worship

In the interviews both lay people and staff members of the case-study churches were asked: "The next set of questions have to do with your view of worship, but before I ask you any questions about worship, please relate to me an experience you have had, that you would consider worship at its best." Here are some representative responses I have organized under headings that, taken as a group, describe what the people in the project say worship is at its best.

1) *There is a sense of immediacy to it.*

a.. An Episcopal priest speaks of the liturgy engaging people in the midst of great personal tragedy:

> One of the most incredible worship services I ever was in-
> volved with was a funeral in 1978. Mother and child were killed by
> a train in Idaho. Only child. And we did the funeral for them, and it
> was a magnificent liturgical experience in which the liturgy spoke to
> and engaged people where they were, and yet helped them put what
> they were feeling in the context of what God and the Christian faith
> is all about. A very powerful service that I think ministered to the
> family and those who were grieving these two untimely deaths.

b. An Episcopal priest describes a lay person making a statement of faith at his baptism:

> I had the privilege of baptizing an adult two weeks ago. A
> man with whom I had been working for a couple of months in prep-
> aration for a baptism. And it was a time of the renewal of baptismal
> vows for the congregation as well as his taking these vows. It was a
> very, very moving experience for me, for him, and for the congrega-
> tion. Many people had not been present at an adult baptism before,
> and this young man made a very moving statement about what it
> meant to him to be baptized. It was a very exciting moment.

2) *There is an experience of the corporate nature of the church.*

a. A United Methodist pastor speaks of the people gathered at her ordination:

The presence of God was very real there. The Body of Christ was so real because it was all those people who had been part of my life and . . . oh, they just extended themselves over and over again for me. Now that doesn't go back to my earliest childhood, but still, you might say that those people were like the people in my growing up years in the church because they were the Body of Christ, the living presence of God for me. They made it all real to me. And they were a wonderful family for me, too. All came together there, all the people who participated and who attended.

b. A United Methodist choir director tells of the congregation working together:

Worship [[at its best is worship] which engages the people who are there: one wonderful way was a time in which we were talking about the saints of the church and the fact that all of us, the children as well as the adults, were saints. We spent that Sunday around the whole idea of saints, singing about it, and talking about it, and writing the names of saints, and really thinking and remembering and sharing. Everybody seemed to have a way to participate. That really felt as if we were operating on lots of different levels, but it worked as a community.

3) *It is intimate.*

a. A United Methodist minister of music describes a powerful moment in his life:

I can think of experiences where I would be alone praying with just a small group of people in just a very quiet setting, worshipping, worshipful. And this would be the antithesis of [worship at a huge shrine] but just as meaningful because of the closeness, the sense of intimacy.

b. An Episcopal priest describes the sense of *presence* in a good liturgy:

Liturgy, in my view, ought to be as grand as an opera and as intimate as a kiss. That it ought to be as grand as an opera [means it ought] to enlarge our horizons. We have this magnificent event going on, which you're not just watching but *present* for. And [it should be] so intimate that it touches you in a very deep place, as intimate as a kiss might be.

4) *It is personally relevant.*

a. A United Methodist laywoman speaks of Holy Communion and then makes a connection between the purpose of a particular worship act and her own grief:

> Communion on Sunday where I feel that I have the chance to come to the altar and talk to God personally and ask forgiveness for my sins and thank Him for all that He has given me. Let me see . . . one worship in particular: I love it when we have the memorial service for the veterans and the Legion people. They love coming here to our church—they love the music here so—and I think that it helps them to mourn, which is good, and so we do what they want, every year. For them, we do the taps, we sing it, and we play it on the trumpet. I particularly like that one; I suppose it's because I've had a lot of deaths in my family and maybe I'm still mourning myself.

b. A United Methodist laywoman describes the preaching in her church:

> Some of Hal's sermons have really been that way for me because I think he's tailor-made for our family. We went through a very difficult time with my stepson. [Finally] I told my husband, "I need some support!" and I called Hal, and he was there for us immediately. He   came and spent a long time talking one night. We came to church the next Sunday and there was a sermon on "Yet another story about a prodigal son." And I know that was very tailor-made to our family. . . . That was a way of the church showing me how supportive and caring they are. At the same time it was very meaningful for anybody.

5) *The components of the liturgy are integrated.*

a. An organist in a United Methodist church describes an experience of coherent worship:

It just means most to me when it all hangs together; and it maybe even will work out—maybe I wouldn't know in advance—that one of the hymns, the text from the liturgy, and the anthem may all be using the same text.

On the subject of the integration of music and liturgy around a common theme or text there was one very strong dissenter, a lay leader from the same church:

I don't think a service has to be homogeneous. A lot of people who worship think you've got to have everything pointing to one central theme. All the songs are one idea, and everything points—I don't believe in that. I believe that as long as you provide a variety of ways for people to think about God, that's what's important, rather than having something that's all planned towards one conclusion. That may run counter to current theory of how sermons and worships are put together, but that's the way I feel about it. I don't like to be managed. When it comes out all one way, I'm managed. I don't like it!

* * * * * * * * * *

These people described what for them have been "peak experiences" connected in some way with worship. They spoke of being unified within themselves, with one another, and with God. Many of them experienced some sort of transformation; and for an overwhelming majority of them these experiences were accompanied by deep feeling.

In all of these instances, people are speaking of heightened experience. In this, their reports are consistent with the results of the questionnaire, where 54 percent of the entire sample agree that the most important reason they come to worship is the *experience* enjoyed there: "I enjoy the feeling of meditating and communicating with God." People in the sample come to worship mainly because something happens there, not out of a sense of duty or because it is seen as instrumental to some other experience. In some cases, the experiences reported are put within a larger context: the Christian faith, the communion of saints, the gathered community, the Body of Christ. They have individual and corporate dimensions.

Worship on an Ordinary Sunday

Most people in the above accounts are speaking of the high points, the great worship moments in their lives, and, as we all know, these do not occur every Sunday. The following accounts are taken from laypeople immediately after worship on an ordinary Sunday. Here a somewhat more mundane picture emerges. The responses are organized again under five descriptive headings.

1) Taking one's place in God's order

In one Episcopal church, coming to church for worship was a way of taking one's appointed place in the order of God's plan for God's people and for the world. What happened there was in some ways irrelevant; that it happened, is happening, and will happen in the future and that one is faithful to it are of primary importance.

a. Here is a lay person talking about worship that Sunday in this church:

> I've heard these things so many times, it's second nature to me. I don't think after all these years that you—what do I want to say—have any special meaning for it, except that it is part of the service, and you go right along and follow right along. It's hard to express my feelings about some of these things. It's been part of me all my life, so it's just that I enjoy doing it.

b. The head usher that morning reports his experience:

> You pay attention, and yet you don't. Your mind will wander, you'll see something else or maybe the sun will shine in through the window and make a pretty light and you'll look there, and you forget all about [the reader]. One of the Smith children, the small one, was running back and forth. She's a little bitty girl. She runs downstairs . . . and I'm afraid she's going to fall, and the mother just isn't, she's not a bit nervous about it, and I don't know why because it is a little tot, you know, she'd go bouncing down those steps and then we'd have a heck of a problem. So you watch that, and your mind wanders off of what's going on at the altar for a minute. But then, to be truthful . . . I

mean if you come to church every Sunday, you know just about what's going to happen, and then if your mind wanders, *if you come back and you see that everything's all right, and you can— I can almost say word for word what he's saying.*

[Interviewer] Tune right back in, yeah.

Yeah, so you don't miss too much. Maybe you miss the meanings of some of the readings. Because, like I say, you don't pay that much attention. *But you don't lose the meaning of the service itself.* [Emphasis added]

2. *Using it as a springboard for self-examination or musings*

   a. A United Methodist laywoman speaks of the confession:

   Well, I was especially cognizant of the "Forgive our sin of separation" because I think we all get separated between church services, separated from worship, from praise, from showing our love for each other, from living a Christian life. We are so caught up in busy things. There are not enough hours in the day for doing the Lord's work. I'm a guilty party, too.   But . . . it brings to mind the things that I should be doing that I don't do. So I just try to examine myself at that time.

   b. An Episcopal layman responds to a reading from John 21 with a "flight of fancy":

   I'm a scientist and I certainly perk up my ears at [the number] 153. I don't know—why 153? You know, I've heard over the years about—I'll call it numerology—numbers that might mean something. It didn't occur to me that 153 could be the number of fish. I mean, in other cultures a certain number means uncountable—that 153 would mean an uncountable number of fish. I think I was struck about why Jesus was cooking fish, but then asked for additional fish. And where did the fish come from that he had been cooking on the charcoal fire?

3) *Thinking leading to action*

   a. A United Methodist laywoman talks about her response to the end of worship:

No particular response. Well, except that Ron did say, "Now
let us go forth." And I try to go forth as much as I can. I'm 83
years old, by the way, but I'm still driving and Monday I'm going
to take the woman who used to be the organist at St. Matthew's
church . . . to the doctor. Tuesday I'm going to drive another
woman. So I'm trying to go forth because of the many wonderful
things that happened to me. I'm a very fortunate person.

4) *Spontaneous petition and prayer*

a. An Episcopal laywoman speaks of being affected by the music
in her church:

We generally have at least a Gloria of some kind, depending
on the season of the year. All during Lent we sang a version of
Psalm 92, "Create in me a clean heart, O God, and renew a right
spirit within me." We generally have that, and then at least two or
three praise songs because this church is a charismatic church, and
praise is very important for leaving the world behind and getting
into the right frame of mind to be really worshipping. I wasn't
expecting it to be this emotional type of. . . . This particular set of
songs really triggered something in me. I don't know if you saw
me. I was the person who started praying about "Please, come
back." I think part of the reason it happened to me is that I have
been reading some books by Charles Williams, who was a friend
of C. S. Lewis, and who writes these amazing novels of supernatu-
ral mystery, and I had just finished reading one of his called *Many
Dimensions*. And there is a lot of immanence in them. [She
pauses.] My life is a very satisfying life, but there are just some
times when I just start yearning for all this . . . this hard work and
striving and all this stuff, to be over! Finished! Done for everybody!

5) *A pattern for weekday devotion*

a. A United Methodist laywoman speaks about saying the Lord's
Prayer:

I say it every day, anyway. Sometimes at night, sometimes

in the morning, whenever. . . . Maybe I'm not the person you
should contact because for the last year, I have been under doctors,
five or six doctors. And I'm so cognizant of the Lord, and the
promises, and the happiness, and the love that surrounded me at
the time when I was the sickest. But I am prejudiced.

[Interviewer]: So was that something that you especially felt
during the Lord's Prayer then?

No, I'm afraid that repeating the Lord's Prayer in church is
sort of a . . . you just do it. When I say it at night, nobody's press-
ing me to [say it]. [She speaks very quickly:] "Thy will be done
on earth as it is in heaven." You know, that sort of thing. [Her
pace becomes more measured:] "Thy will be done on earth," I
mean, you stop [and ask]: "How is His will done and should be
done on earth? And "as it is in heaven" how some day it will be
[done]. So that the Lord's Prayer at home means a lot more to me
than the Lord's Prayer at church, aside from the fact that we are all
saying it together.

* * * * * * * * *

This set of interview responses reinforces and enlarges upon the
sense of present time in the first set. Worship is described in the context
of people's everyday lives. However, its meaning stretches out in two
directions: to the past—as people take their places in God's order, re-
established for them through the discipline of common worship, daily
prayer, and mission; and to the future—with its promise of the coming to
earth of the Reign of God, seen through ecstatic vision of the Eschaton as
well as in the little things people do for one another.

Responses such as these provide those in leadership positions with
information about the way people appropriate the ingredients of worship
that they find when they come to church on Sunday. Even though they
are occupied in similar ways (and, with the Episcopalians, with identical
texts), the meaning of what they do varies from week to week and from
place to place. These people are Episcopalians and United Methodists
from one region of the country. The specific claims that they make may
or may not sound familiar to others. However, this *type* of information is
essential to those whose responsibility is the planning of weekly worship.

When Things Go Wrong

The research teams who visited the eight case-study churches were sent to take part in worship on an "ordinary" Sunday. The staff of each church were not informed when the team's visit would occur, and the people contacted to be interviewed after worship were cautioned to remain silent about the impending visit.

In their reports, each team was asked to make a value statement about what they had encountered. Four of the eight reported that the experience had been powerful and engaging. Of the four congregations where worship seemed less effective and engaging, two services were reported in total chaos.

At the group interview of one of the churches whose worship was chaotic, the staff discussed that particular Sunday:

> [Interviewer] "The rector spoke about [the problem of] attentiveness. This was as a result of the—the lector didn't have the papers, and there was only one acolyte and several things. . . ."
> "That was the day. . . ."
> "The second time he acolyted exactly the same thing happened the other. . . ."
> "Right, nobody showed up, and this was. . . ."
> "That was the service where all of us left."
> "That was the one where everything, everything. . . ."
> "Everybody left. I had to leave, you left."
> "Right. We were chasing him all over the place."
> "We were chasing him down, the service was just running itself, and we were just. . . ."
> "And that's right, and all of a sudden out of nowhere, [the rector] came back and we were down there wondering. . . ."
> "Were you doing ice cream?"
> "I did the ice cream with the kids downstairs, that's right."

Every church has an occasional Sunday like the one described above! Yet such chaos on a weekly basis can have an adverse effect on a worshipping community. In one church, chaos was spawned out of the conflict between the pastor and the rest of the staff, particularly the musicians. Everyone was functioning on his or her own with little or no communication and support from the others. The competition was immediately evident to the visiting team. I will return to this church's situation in the chapter on planning.

Music in Worship

The cumulative effect of reading these interviews is powerful. Indeed they were powerful as they took place. Of course these people knew that they were going to be asked questions about worship in their churches, so they were primed. On an ordinary Sunday, I would imagine that quite a lot of "wool-gathering" goes on. Yet the interviews show a deep level of religious commitment and understanding among ordinary churchgoers.

These testimonies and descriptions point to why music is so frequently used in worship. What better means of establishing a corporate sense of immediacy than through such a participatory act as singing? Because art is an event that draws people into it, it fosters personal appropriation on the part of the singer or player. It serves to connect people to their pasts as well as to those standing around them by releasing memory and feeling. It inspires people to act, a reality to which the great civil rights marches of the past decades attest.

One of the primary functions of music in worship is to undergird and make articulate the individual and corporate faith of the congregation. Thus, one of the first responsibilities of anyone coming into a new congregation as its music director is to listen to the people talk about their faith and the way in which worship exemplifies it. The staff is accountable to the congregation in this instance, to its faith life and its musical vocabulary. Every congregation has a culture or cultures: a local tradition, a set of practices and repertory that exemplifies its faith. It has a voice, or voices, that the music on Sunday releases. The leaders of the congregation need to know this voice—the feelings and attitudes it exemplifies and reinforces. They should share an understanding of worship and its local manifestation in their congregation. What does this particular set of practices tell us about this community and its people? How do people in this congregation describe what goes on in worship? What draws them here on Sunday?

CHAPTER 3

Singing in Church

Introduction

In the preceding chapter, we heard people talking about worship. In this
chapter and the next, we will examine their views about both congregational singing and about the choir.

An elderly gentleman of grand stature and poise stood at the door
of the very first church I entered to pass out questionnaires for the project. When I explained who I was and what I was there for, he exclaimed,
"Is this where I get to write that I want to sing 'The Little Brown Church
in the Vale'?" I laughed and said, "Yes! Here you can write about anything you want!"

The subject of singing in church evoked passion, enthusiasm, and,
yes, even anger everywhere the project team went. This ordinary act of
singing in church provoked extraordinary responses, which again points
to the importance of music to the life of faith of most churchgoers. In
chapter 1, I gave a detailed philosophical explanation of the way music
and faith connect. Chapters 3 and 4 approach the same issue, although
more indirectly, through a thorough look at the findings about congregational singing and about the choir. These reports of the congregations
and choirs in the twenty-four churches provide concrete information
about this all-important connection. They clothe the principles in flesh-
and-blood and suggest practical solutions to problems that many church
musicians and pastors face.

The Power of Hymn Singing

Asked why she picked a particular hymn as her favorite, a woman responded, "It sounds the way following Christ is like!" This statement expresses in very few words the relationship between hymn singing and faith. For this woman her favorite hymn functions as a symbol of what living a life of faith is like! Singing it among her friends on a Sunday morning enlivens her faith because she manifests it in the singing. Music is an event in which the life embodied in the art work and the life of the beholder or performer meet. As a community sings "Were You There When They Crucified My Lord?" it journeys back to that hillside so vividly captured in the Christian imagination and relives the faith that that image has carried throughout the ages.

The capacity of a community's song to carry the faith of its members helps to explain an important finding in the project. Because music evokes such a powerful response it takes on or retains the characteristics of the people who are stirred by it. Congregations develop repertories and styles of singing all their own. Thus one community's song may not be another's. *In other words, church music programs are not necessarily interchangeable!* What is a lively symbol of faith in one group may be a meaningless one in another.

I do not mean to imply by this statement that congregations have nothing in common and therefore generalization is fruitless. I do mean to add a note of caution: It is risky to generalize about anything that taps so deeply into the ethos of a people as music does.

Musical Lives of Congregations

Having pointed out the power of singing in church and the pitfalls of coming to easy conclusions about the musical lives of a particular group, I turn now to the section on music in the questionnaire. In the list below, the first figure represents the entire sample. The figures in parentheses represent cases where the two denominations (Episcopal and United Methodist) are significantly different.

    32%   consider themselves musicians (E36;M29)
    64%   read music (E68;M60)
    44%   play musical instruments

16% are involved in musical activities outside the church

26% have participated in formal or informal group singing outside the church in the last six months

57% say that the music program in their church is very important to them (E51;M62)

61% favor increasing the resources for music in their churches

57% rank hymns as the most important aspect of music in worship (E65;M51)

40% rank anthems as the second most important aspect of music in worship (E42;M58)

When ranking themselves as singers:

50% said they like to sing but don't do it well
46% said they like to sing and do it well

Finally, congregational singing and the choice of hymns receive the most complaints from both the people surveyed and those interviewed.–
Several things stand out in these statistics:

1) Hymn singing is very important to people.
2) Half the people who sing don't think they do it well.
3) More than half of them can read music.
4) For three–quarters of them church *is the only place they get to sing in a group or at all!* As   Horace T. Allen once remarked in a discussion about the pervasiveness of television in our culture, "Worship on Sunday morning may be America's last live act!"
5) Over half of the people are willing to *increase* the resources allocated for music programs in their churches.

These responses deserve comment because they provide often overlooked information needed to plan music for congregational singing. For example, methods of teaching new hymns would differ depending on on whether or not one's congregation considered themselves good singers. Also, if church is the only place people get the opportunity to sing, those in charge might have to coax them into participation and work over a long period of time to nurture hesitant singers to join in with vigor and enthusiasm.

Complaints About Hymns

The complaints about the choice of hymns and about congregational singing also deserve longer discussion. I encountered a lot of anger about the hymns people are given to sing on Sunday morning. People want to sing the "old hymns" which seem to be their favorites, hymns of an earlier generation such as "What a Friend We Have in Jesus" and "O Master, Let Me Walk with Thee." These requests from people in the congregation set off minor explosions among clergy and church musicians, many of whom see this as evidence of theological naivete and lack of taste among their constituents. Because this argument is both pervasive and predictable, I lay out here a broader view, based on the results of the project.

Views of the Congregation

One of the most striking things uncovered in the interviews of lay people in the case study churches was their desire to be immersed in music making. In the interviews I asked them what they would do if they found themselves Church Musician for the Week. Their dreams took many forms. One main raised in England wanted to pass out copies of *his* favorite hymns (from the English Methodist tradition) so that the people around him could experience the fullness of faith in his tradition. Another wanted to import a local college choir that regularly "raised the roof" so that the people in her congregation could have the same experience she had. Another wanted to bring back *The Hymnal 1940* so that congregational singing would be revived. Another wanted to rip out the sanctuary and build another so that the acoustics would support the organ and congregational singing. Another wanted to bring the congregation up into the midst of the choir so that they could experience the joy that such singing could bring. In all of these responses, one sees a desire to be saturated with music.

The recognition of the spiritual power of music making and a hunger for it often lies behind the desire to sing the "old hymns." They are full of meaning for people who have been using them for decades to express faith. Yet to outsiders who are not privy to this experience, they may appear shabby and out of date. Another aspect of this question of the "old hymns" pertains to the quality of participation in familiar music.

People remarked over and over again on the importance to them of the
Gloria Patri and the *Doxology*. Indeed, one research team reported that
the only time there was any visible sign of life in their congregation
occurred at the singing of the *Doxology* that accompanied the Offertory
procession. With familiar music, people put down their books and sing
their hearts out.

In contrast to that experience, unfamiliar music can cause them
problems. Here is one woman describing the singing of a new hymn:

> That was a completely new one for me. Yes, that was the one that
> had two different versions, the single line and the harmony one.
> And I got mixed up halfway through the second verse. I kept
> saying, "Which one am I supposed to sing?" And that was a
> distraction to me—interestingly enough—although I do remember
> singing it, and enjoying it, and liking it. But then being distracted
> when I thought I was going down and somebody else was going
> up. I thought, "Oh, I don't care! I'll just do my way!" Nobody
> hears me sing anyway, although I always sing, and I'm always part
> of a group; but I don't stand out.

Earlier in the interview, this same woman remarked that she had
gotten to church too late to sing *the* familiar hymn this Sunday. She
liked having a balance between the familiar and the new.

Control over what goes on in the worship life of a congregation is
also a factor in the debate about the "old hymns." One man involved in
the pilot project wrote me a long note on the back of the original version
of the questionnaire offering suggestions for modification:

> This questionnaire is all right as far as it goes but it ignores
> some crucial issues:
>
> 1) Church music and the unity and coherence of the service.
> 2) The relative autonomy of the choir director and/or
>   organist.
> 3) The function of anthems.
> 4) Whether foreign languages should be used by soloists
>   and the choir without the translation being provided the
>   worshipers. In my view the congregation should not
>   only be able to enjoy the music but also be able to enter
>   into the words intelligibly.

5) Whether preludes, postludes, and offertory should be mini-concerts.
6) Whether the "experts" should be in control.
7) Whether the "church year" should control the use and choice of hymns, anthems, type of service, etc.

His views were highly egalitarian. He felt that the music of the church is chiefly the concern of the congregation. In this church, a group of people went to the pastor and voiced complaints about tailoring all the hymns to the theme of the sermon. They agreed that he should choose the sermon hymn yet arranged a structure where their views could influence the choice of the other hymns. Subsequently the pastor solicited a list of the congregation's favorite hymns and, with the help of the organist and worship committee, initiated a Hymn Sing before the service on the second Sunday of the month where people could call out their hymn requests.

Views of the Staff

Musicians and clergy work to bring both aesthetic and theological coherence to worship on Sunday morning. This entails scrutiny of the texts of hymns and anthems to support the lessons and the various components of Sunday's prayer and praise. Here is one church musician talking about the work he does to prepare for Sunday:

> The principal item on the agenda [of the weekly staff meeting] is liturgical planning. By way of background, I have done my musical planning, including hymn selections, anthem selections, organ music, and service music. I have thought a good deal about that and tried to relate them to the themes of the day as defined by the Propers [the readings assigned for that Sunday]. And on the other hand, the preacher has also come to the meeting with a pretty good notion of what he or she would be preaching about, based again on the Propers of the Day. And then we sit around a table and talk about all this, and we talk about it at some length. And out of that process, I think hardly ever does a liturgy that takes place on Sunday exactly reflect what my plans were. I mean, it usually would be some hymn change or some alteration for very

good reasons, and I'm happy to partake of that exchange and that interchange of ideas.

Later on in the interview he talked about a more subtle form of musical planning for the Sunday liturgy:

> Both the assistant organist and I try to plan organ music that in some way is consistent with a kind of a theme for the day. I very often find it hard to define what this aesthetic theme is. There may be various different composers from various different periods involved in a given service. But in order for that to work for me, I've got to justify it not only in lectionary terms but in aesthetic terms. That continuity, that line is hard to get, but when it comes it seems natural to me.

Another choir director had this to say about planning:

> The organist and I plan . . . together weekly. We spend time on the phone; we spend Tuesday mornings here. The first thing I do is I go through a season of the year with the lectionary and live with the texts for a while, and then I choose anthems that I feel we can deal with. Then I bring those to Sue, and we talk about them, and we look at the music together. There we have rules that we like to follow. The text comes first and then next comes style; within a six-week period hopefully [there will be] a variety of styles and also instrumentation, choir and congregation. And the children sing one time—a combination so that it becomes an inclusive pattern."

The Argument Examined

Baldly stated, the argument between the two sides is this: those in a position to choose hymns for worship pick out those that follow principles of good worship design; congregations want to sing hymns they are familiar with. Behind the apparent disagreement lies a similar value: *coherence.* For their part, clergy and musicians work to knit together the parts of the service and the lessons for theological reasons and to bring shape to the time spent on Sunday morning. They are sensitive to the power that such coherence lends to communicating the gospel—the "good news." For example, choosing as the last hymn one that picks up the theme of the sermon and sends people forth into the world reinforces the message and gives people energy to carry it into their lives beyond the sanctuary.

The congregation is also interested in coherence but of a different sort, having to do with the fabric of their lives. They bring the wealth of their past religious experience into the sanctuary every Sunday. The "old hymns" are icons that provide the means to reconnect to and transform that experience in light of the present day. For example, singing "The Old Rugged Cross" after a sermon on the perseverance of people as they work to provide shelter for the homeless attaches all the past meaning brought with the hymn to a present-day mission concern. What one knows of perseverance in the past now can inform the response to the sermon.

The former sort of coherence has to do with the event itself; the latter has to do with the meaning that that event has in the lives of the congregation as a whole and the worshipers as individuals. Sensitivity to the shape of worship is also common to both views. As many know, the opening hymn gathers the community together. This function is best served by a familiar hymn that lets the people "cohere." Through exuberant singing, the worries of the week and the hassle of getting the kids out of the house that morning are put aside. An unfamiliar hymn at this point in the service could disrupt the purpose of the gathering.

In reality both views point to things essential to good worship. Once defensiveness and hostility are lessened and good patterns of communication established, congregations can develop patterns that honor both views.

Kind of Music Used in Worship

Question 34 asked: "Which of the following statements comes the closest to your view of the *kind* of music to be used in worship?" Here are the two choices which were selected most frequently:

> 47% said that "any kind of music is appropriate as long as the congregation can use it to praise God."
> 24% said that "since music in worship is an offering to God, only the best is appropriate."

In the first statement, the function of music in worship is stressed. Any music can be used so long as it is an adequate vehicle for the praise of God. In the second statement criteria of excellence are introduced: "only the best." In the question itself, there is no attempt to define what "the best" is or who gets to make that judgment. Indeed, someone might argue that only the best music has the *capacity* to function as praise to God. Inferior music by definition cannot perform that function. It might be a form of praise of, say, American consumerism but not of God. (The questionnaire was inadequate for gauging the more subtle aspects of this argument. The case studies were undertaken partly as an antidote for the distortions of quantifiable data.)

One might assume that those who are drawn to participate in choirs or other musical organizations in the church would consider criteria of excellence to take precedence over other considerations. However, one's membership in the adult choir of one's church is not a significant factor in the answers. (The use of the word "significant" here pertains to whether the figures are *statistically* significant.)

What is a significant factor is the age of the respondent. Those 51 and over (the median age of the sample) chose the second of the two options at a higher percentage and those under 51 chose the first at a higher percentage. In other words, of the 372 people who chose the first option, 57% were under 51 and 43% were 51 or over. Of the 186 people who chose the second option, only 25% were under 51. Seventy-five per cent were 51 or older. This pattern held true across denominational lines.

The data from other parts of the survey suggest that this functional attitude toward music among younger people is linked to a change in the view about what constitutes church affiliation and what it means to be religious. People older than the median age chose "attending worship" and "receiving Holy Communion" when asked when they felt closest to God. Those people younger than the median chose "helping individuals in need," "walking by the sea," and "small prayer groups." When asked about their religious practices, the younger people tended to do the following with greater frequency than the older people: "read or study the bible with friends or as part of a group," "share religious beliefs with others who have *similar* beliefs," "share religious beliefs with those who have *different* beliefs," "pray with members of family or friends other than Grace [at meals]." (Here again I am working with differences that are statistically significant.) Although one cannot say, based on the results of the survey, that younger people lack interest in formal worship, their responses reflect a broadening in their religious practices and interests. Small groups—bible study, consciousness raising, self-help, 12-step programs—with their egalitarian and informal structure are often their milieu.

Robert Wuthnow in *The Restructuring of American Religion* devotes an entire chapter to the growth in popularity of what he terms "special purpose groups" and traces their history within American religion over the last two centuries. He says of them,

> They focus on limited objectives, attract participants with special interests, and generally do not constitute the main arenas in which the worship and instruction of the church as a corporate body take place. [The bible study group would have to be exempted from this description.] Sometimes they are local chapters of larger organizations within the denomination. But often they have no connection at all with the activities of other churches [988:108].

It will take more research to document what effects if any the shift in religious practice among younger people has on Sunday worship. Some hint of it shows up in the answers to Question 43, the pictographs of worship at its best. [See Appendix A for this diagram.] Those people who chose the more formal and hierarchical postures, the people kneeling and the preacher (1, 5, and 6), tended to be older than the median age of the sample. Those who chose the more egalitarian and informal posture, the circle of people holding hands, tended to be younger than the median age.

Conclusion

Much of the music included in worship is designed for congregations to perform. This goes for hymns and liturgical responses. What are the musical capacities of the congregation? Is the music chosen sung well? If not, why not? These questions harken back to the question about efficiency posed at the beginning of the book. Much of worship is carried through congregational singing. Is this activity done well? Is it functioning the way it should? Or is the music given the congregation trivialized, either because it makes no liturgical sense or because few enter into the experience?

A student of mine working in a Roman Catholic church embarked on an educational program under the guise of the "Hymn of the Month." Throughout the course of a year, he taught a series of unfamiliar hymns to his congregation in a variety of ways—through the creative use of the choir as support, historical notes in the newsletter, and brief descriptions in the Sunday bulletin. This pursuit had a much broader effect than an increase of twelve new hymns to the congregational repertory. Because someone was taking both time and trouble to focus on the hymns being sung by the congregation, *all* the hymn singing became stronger. His care spoke volumes about the importance of the activity of hymn singing.

No matter what one's view is of any of the controversial questions about hymns and styles of worship, there can be no doubt that the project results pointed out the need and desire to pay more attention to congregational singing. This situation calls for increased emphasis on the educational role of the church musician. Congregations are filled with people whose musical lives consist in singing in church, *period!* Electronic media, while giving people access to music beyond the performance capacities of local music groups, have narrowed performing opportunities. Now with concert ticket prices at exorbitant rates, live performances are luxuries for most people, as is time to join performing groups for many working people. Music programs in private and public schools are being cut back or eliminated altogether because of budget restraints. How one nourishes the singing voice of the congregation has widespread importance not only for the worship life of each local church but for the arts in the wider society.

When planning is done, are the capacities and deficiencies of the congregation taken into consideration? Are their abilities being expanded? What is the singing voice of the congregation like? And how about the Sunday School? Are children being taught the hymns of the faith?

ENDNOTES

Wuthnow, Robert. *The Restructuring of American Religion.* Princeton, N.J.: Princeton University Press, 1988.

CHAPTER 4

The Choir

Introduction

In Chapter 3 I focused on congregational singing; here I turn my attention to the choir. The existence of choirs in churches is something we all take for granted, yet their establishment as a regular feature of worship has not always been assured. In the past, choirs have been disbanded and instruments destroyed for their purported bad influences on the faith of the gathered people. Mixed feelings about the choir persist today, even in such tranquil times as ours when people are no longer burned at the stake for advocating liturgical change. The data from the project provide information about this ambivalence, as well as strong documentation for the persistence of choirs and people's love for them.

Choirs and Their Advocates

Choirs existed in seven of the eight case-study churches of the project. The eighth church occasionally brought together a group of people to sing for special services, but maintained that the congregation itself functioned as the choir for the most part, making the special group somewhat redundant. These choirs ran the gamut in size, presence of paid singers, budget, and repertory. The smallest had four singers in it, all volunteers; the largest ranged to about thirty with ten paid soloists. They shared three things: enthusiasm, commitment, and hard work.

A choir member in a suburban church spoke in enthusiastic terms about the music program in her church and the role of the choir in it:

Music should enhance worship; it should be inspiring. It makes it so much more meaningful. It makes me feel closer to God. The music program here is always appropriate, well done, and challenging. I go to choir because I like it. I think we are very important; we are leaders in the church body. I think we provide definite leadership for a lot of people there. I think if we were not there, I would hope we would be sadly missed. What David [the choir director] does is definitely a form of ministry. He knows his music so well, and music to me is essential to worship. He has a very rich background, and I appreciate singing for him.

When asked to describe the music program in this church the director of music spoke most frequently about the choir:

I think the standards are remarkably high. And those high standards have been maintained by the last two organists and myself in the absence of any paid singers. There's a long-standing tradition that we don't pay anyone to sing, almost no matter what. And I think that's an unusual thing. To stage a program in which you sing —as we do on a regular basis—close to 100 different anthems in the course of a year, plus at least one major choral or another kind of cantata "thing" in the spring, without the support of paid people, is kind of unusual, I think—despite the fact that the choir itself really calls for quality. There are a number of things this choir has told people—luckily, they've never said this to me—but they have said to other people, that this [piece of music] simply will not do. The quality of this music is just not high enough for us. That's unusual. Other qualities about the music program? Again, I keep coming back to the choir because it is a unique group of individuals. Its steadfastness is impressive. Through thick and thin, this group keeps showing up and have kept showing up through some very difficult periods in the history of the church. Very often in my experience, the people in the choir are somehow or other compartmentalized away from the rest of the church. It's not true here. We have wardens and vestrymen and heads of Episcopal Church Women and all that kind of stuff in the choir. In fact, part of the danger in this church is that you're not going to be anybody unless you're a member of the choir. And that's one of the things we've got to watch out for.

The organist in another church made these observations about her choir:

> The choir is such an important part of this church. Many
> people, for a long time, thought the choir is the place to belong. In
> fact, we have some people who really don't sing too well, but they
> just like the community of the choir. They are a very caring com-
> munity. I take charge of birthday parties for the group, and I'm in
> charge of organizing the parties. And I try and visit the people in
> the choir when they're sick or go see them about things. Being the
> organist is being a part of the choir—it's sort of like a small church
> in itself.

Enthusiasm for choirs is not limited to their members:

> The choir in this church is without peer. We have been to
> churches with twice as many, and most of them—remember that
> most of these people are in the Pops concert and have been rehears-
> ing since January, in addition to doing the church choir, the bell
> choir, the junior choir—and you just have to admire them for their
> fortitude and their dedication and persistence and all. And their
> talent. And there are some days, they just lift you, blow you right
> away. They just seem to love it as much as we love listening to it.
> And last Sunday they had one of Sally's sisters' husband in the
> choir, and he played the trumpet, and they sang their hearts out. Oh,
> it was just beautiful! And of course, the trumpet helped. And so
> when they got all through, I said, from my seat here in the congrega-
> tion, "Don't you think we should give them a round of applause?"
> And we did. Everybody just felt like, you know, their hearts were
> bursting, and they wanted to do something to show their apprecia-
> tion.

What glowing accounts! But as anyone who has ever picked up a choir
folder would agree, they cannot match the actual experience. Singing
in a choir at times approaches the sublime. Choirs at their best are close-
knit communities that enhance not only the work and worship of the
church but the spiritual and social lives of their members as well.

The Role of the Choir in Worship

Surprisingly, among all those interviewed, I found virtual unanimity in the views about how choirs should function in worship. Choirs provide leadership for the worship of the congregation. One choir director put it this way:

> I always tell my choir, they are singing to the glory of God; therefore, I don't want anybody in those choir stalls giving a performance. They're saying prayers for the congregation. They're asking for the congregation through their music. And I always tell them to forget everything else. Just keep that and don't be afraid of making mistakes. Don't let it scare you be- cause we all make mistakes, and God understands we're not doing it on purpose. And the rest is going to take care of itself, and it does. And I like that the congregation has noticed that that's happened. They said everything seems to mesh together and they also tell me that they like the choir because I said "You're sup- posed to be giving them a message. Enunciate your words. Let them know what you're talking about." I said, "You need notes and you need words, but it's up to you to interpret it."

The choir director with the professional singers had a different view. He emphasized the leadership function of the choir but expanded it to include the notion of performance:

> The choir has a performance function which I say proudly be- cause there's nothing worse than having—I wouldn't know from *personal* experience—but [there's] nothing worse than having a Porsche and then making it drive fifteen miles an hour all the time. We have some really fine singers here, and I think the point is to use them well for the service of the worship in this parish. So the choir has a performance role *and* a leadership role, leadership in the service music and the hymn singing.

Problems

The problems each of these choirs faced were also similar: recruitment of personnel, attendance at rehearsals, and the tendency of the choir to split off from the congregation.

In one church the aggressive recruitment for the choir was half-jokingly cited as the reason the congregation was singing poorly. The choir director said:

> I've been accused of recruiting anybody who comes in the church building who can sing. So it doesn't leave voices in the congregation. I have, and we do! When we process and recess, all of us are listening to the new people who are in the congregation. If there's a voice there, we pick up on them right away.

Another choir director bemoaned the lack of resources for the music program:

> The biggest problem in our musical program has been the lack of people involved. The largest number of choir members has been the people most of whom do not read music. At special services, we have invited outside churches to participate and it has worked out well. Outside activities on Sunday morning have played a large part in the loss of people who could take part in choir service.

Attendance at rehearsals was particularly a problem in churches whose constituencies were drawn from the "high tech" industry. One choir director described his method of planning to compensate for erratic attendance:

> I do my choral planning generally two to three to four months in advance. I issue long repertoire lists which I Xerox and every-body in the choir gets one to put up on their refrigerator door, so that they know three months in advance what the anthems are. I do this, not so much to be inflexible, but actually to make sure that I've got copies. And, in a parish in which lots of folks, in the choir espe-cially, are movers and shakers and all the time running around the world, it's really necessary that everything that's going to be done in church, gets into rehearsal six weeks before the time that it goes on

the boards. That at least gives me one crack at most of the people who will be singing it. It'll give me six weeks with half the choir, three weeks with another third, and so on and so forth. But everybody, at any rate, will have seen the piece. I know of no other way to work in that kind of wealthy suburban situation.

Concerning the third problem, that of the choir detaching itself from the congregation, one woman remarked:

> I think the congregation needs more practice in singing, and we need to be taught by these two musicians we have on our paid staff. They're good teachers, but they don't spend any time teaching anybody who's not in the choir. And I have problems with that. I'd like to learn some of these things too, but I don't care to be in the choir. . . . And I'm not objecting to a choir singing anthems and that kind of stuff, but I think when they sing the services, to the exclusion of the congregation, that's a mistake. I want to be able to participate. That happens on what are for me the most important holidays, Easter and Christmas. The congregation gets to sing some Easter hymns and Christmas carols. But the real guts of the situation, we're just observing; we don't see it, we don't participate or sing in it at all.

Another lay person, after a glowing report on the music program in his church, voiced some reservations about the way the choir functioned.

> I think that while we do well in music here, in a sense our *doing* in music is not shared in the same sense as sermons are shared. The participation in hymn singing, for instance, is formal and somewhat impersonal, and there is some separateness between the choir and the congregation in the area of music. It's something like a class system. Not a *caste* system, but a *class* system, because people in the choir are very active in other areas. Also, in other areas of the church, they don't keep to themselves in any sense. But in one way the music of the church is theirs.

Results from the Questionnaire

What can be added to these testimonies about the choirs to explain their functioning in a local church? I have extracted questionnaire answers from those people who had been members of adult choirs in the twenty-four churches in the last five years and compared their responses to all others. Of the 835 people who filled out the questionnaire, 31.6% are or had been choir members.

Musical Lives

As one would predict, choir members are much more musical than their peers in the sample. They are more likely to read music, play instruments, be involved in outside musical organizations, and think they sing well. The music program in their church is vastly more important to them. They consider the anthem a "more meaningful" part of worship than the hymns, whereas the others consider hymns "more meaningful." They rate the music program in their church *somewhat* higher than the others but *clearly* rate the quality of the sermon and ritual lower. As was shown in Chapter 3, they essentially agree with their peers that "any kind of music is appropriate [to worship] as long as the congregation can use it to praise God."

The answers of the two groups to question 35 (see Appendix A) which deals with "frequently voiced statements about church music programs" are reproduced below. There is surprising unanimity between the two groups on this question. The only real disagreement exists in the arena of control of the music program (see statement 8 of quesion 35). Choir members strongly disagree that a committee consisting of staff and lay leaders should have control over the music program. Again it is not clear from the answers to this question who they think *should* have control over it. They "mildly agree" that the director of music should choose the hymns and "mildly disagree" that the minister should choose the hymns. In actual practice among the churches in the project, several planning structures existed, yet more than likely the minister chose the hymns with some consultation with the director of music. Control over the music program is part of the larger issues of the relationship between the choir and the congregation, and the relationship among members of the staff. The former I will treat at length below, the latter in a subsequent chapter, Chapter 6, on planning.

Other Considerations

Choir members in the sample do not differ significantly from their peers
in terms of age, politics, proportion of males and females, educational
level, marital status, etc. They also see the mission of the church in
much the same way as others do. Significant differences between the
two groups crop up in the level and quality of participation in church life.
Choir members attend church functions more regularly; they have more
of their closest friends in the church; they are more likely to have been
"very upset" if they had to leave the particular church; they see their
church as more "closely knit"; and they consider worship to be "very
important" to their ongoing faith lives at a higher percentage. In other
words, their ties to their local church are stronger than the others in the
sample.

These differences in affiliation are reinforced by a tendency to think
in corporate terms about God and the church. Question 42 (see Appendix A) deals with the nature of the church. Respondents were asked to
choose a picture of the interrelationship of God, Jesus Christ, and people.
Among those who chose the view stressing the corporate nature of the
church—"Since the Church is Christ's body and since we, its members,
are the church, together we approach God directly"—choir members
figured at a higher percentage than their numbers in the sample. In other
words, although 31.6% of the sample were choir members, 42.3% of the
people who chose this option were choir members. This tendency also
shows up in the question about attributes of God. Of those who chose
"extremely true" for the phrase "More present in relationships with
others than in an individual's life," 42% were choir members.

Implications of the Data

The implications of these findings for the local congregation are important. Choirs often function at the center of the congregation. They are
very loyal, work hard, and have fun. Added to these strengths is the fact
that they work intimately with an art form of tremendous power. Thus,
not only do they spend a lot of time in church, but what they do there is
very meaningful to their faith lives.

What can other groups within the church learn from the structure
and task of the choir? A student of mine did a research project on

stewardship in his church and found that there was a link between the amount of money given and both the *quantity and the quality* of time given to the church. In other words, people's loyalty to a church grew as their participation grew in both time and substance—and *vice versa.* Building up the Body of Christ consists in providing opportunities for the congregation to take *meaningful* action on behalf of the whole. Campaign speeches from the pulpit may get some response during a stewardship drive; starting a soup kitchen may get some, too!

The Choir as War Department

Unfortunately a choir is not always a beneficial aspect of a parish church. In some instances the choir and the music program can cause divisiveness in a congregation. One of the sayings that circulate among people working in churches and seminaries labels the choir as the "war department."

In several of the case-study churches, tension existed between the choir and the congregation, this in spite of the high regard most people had for the choir director and the choir members as individuals. In one of the churches, outright animosity between the musicians and the clergy accounted for much of the tension. In the other instances, it came from a *perceived* lack of attention (on the part of the choir director or others in charge of worship) to the musical participation of the congregation. Since research team members were in the churches in question only occasionally, it was difficult to evaluate these complaints. What follows is a list of suppositions about the nature of this split based on the observations of the teams.

1. We found that leaders of worship were not good judges of the quality of congregational singing. In many instances, they considered the congregational singing to be better than the team reported it to be. Thus the problem of the congregation's participation was often not even noticed.

2. Choirs develop very strong bonds because of their mutual commitment and dependence on one another. The intensity of feeling that choirs enjoy may create walls that shut out people who do not share this experience, making them feel like outsiders. In this type of situation, opinions about such matters as participation in worship are rarely objective.

3. Because all the new service books and worship manuals place increased emphasis on participation by congregations, they are taking up their new, more active role with enthusiasm. There seems to be a shift away from worship which relied on attentive listening as the main form of participation to a more active "do it ourselves" approach. Standards of participation that were adequate twenty years ago seem too passive today.

4. Sometimes I have thought that this argument between choirs and congregations all boils down to one thing: who gets to have the fun! As the statistics show, choirs find anthems more meaningful and congregations find hymns more meaningful. Musicians enjoy playing music that is increasingly elaborate. Complexity and elaboration are the "stuff" of the well-trained musical imagination. But taken to an extreme, such flights of imagination can leave a congregation sitting on their hands, impatiently watching the show. They want to stand up and belt forth a good, solid hymn at the top of their lungs. Lots of energy is created in good worship, and people want to respond, add to it, and shape it themselves rather than have the professionals do it for them. Conversely, choirs and organists tire of a steady diet of unadorned hymn tunes. They are itching to add a descant, an extraordinary accompaniment, a new arrangement of the text to bring out nuance.

Conclusions

It's clear, simply by the way I have framed the argument, that this is not necessarily an either/or situation. The music of the congregation and the music of the choir are different forms of the same powerful connection, each with its own power and logic. They need not conflict with one another. All agree that the music of the church serves the worship life of the congregation; that is, choir and congregation alike work from the dynamic connection between music and faith. Thus the starting point for any discussion between these two can be their mutual regard for the church at worship.

Many of the questions that are asked of a music program, its director, or staff person in charge, can also be asked of the choir: How does the choir function in worship? To whom is it accountable? This accountability is certainly to the congregation of which it is a leader. Everything that the choir does derives its power from the faith of the community. But there are also other responsibilities that are not as obvious—to the great choral tradition of the church and to musicians like themselves who have stood and will stand in the very choir stalls they now occupy.

During the course of the project, several people remarked that in difficult times the choir had held the church together. Pastors came and went. Serious conflict split the church in myriad ways. Yet, there was that tenacious core of people who, being attached to the experience of singing in worship, persisted in the face of tremendous odds. One might say that choirs like these demonstrate an accountability to the *spirit* of a congregation as well as to the actual congregation.

In most of the project churches, there existed a *tradition* of choirs and choral singing. Present choir directors and choir singers did not have to invent the choir and its role in worship; they received it from their forbears, who had received it from theirs. Carried in this tradition are repertories of music whose performances were also handed down from generation to generation. Singing praise to God is a religious practice that millions of people have participated in and still do. We have an obligation to receive this treasure, tend it lovingly, and pass it on, adding to it that which expresses and forms our faith. It is not ours alone.

CHAPTER 5

The Discipline of Coherence

In Chapters 3 and 4, we looked at the data of the project concerning congregational singing and the choir. The next three chapters will outline ideas and methods concerning the vocation of the church musician.

A church musician's life is ruled by various disciplines: practicing the organ music and the anthems, planning rehearsals, systematically developing a choir's tone, teaching children to sing. Because church musicians do this work behind the scenes, they often find themselves explaining to people what they actually do. Few if any of them show up on Sunday mornings without spending hours in preparation.

I would like to add another—the discipline of coherence. There is a discipline that a church musician develops, along with the technical ones demanded of music makers: that is, there are habits of thought and methods of working that insure that there be coherence between what she or he does and the life of faith of the community served. Coherence means a "natural or logical connection." Its literal definition is "sticking together," but is usually applied figuratively to describe order and consistency of thought. At the end of Chapter 3, we used it to describe an aspect of good worship.

The case studies explore in great depth the meaning of worship and music to the people in a particular congregation and the forms and effectiveness of their music programs. At the center of these case studies are a series of descriptions of worship on one Sunday during the spring of 1989. Included are descriptions by three members of the team and two to three parishioners, an evaluation done by each of the people leading and planning worship that day, and a verbatim transcript of a group interview discussing the theological and practical assumptions of the leaders and the leaders' ratings of their own work. This material is then placed within the context of another set of interviews of people in the church, asking their views of the nature of their church, its worship, and the music program. All in all, each case study provides very detailed information from many different angles about worship one Sunday in these churches.

In looking through all of this material, one of the things I began to notice was the coherence (or lack thereof) of the descriptions of worship on that particular Sunday. When one puts all these partial views together does one picture emerge or many? Does the staff of the church have one idea about what is happening on Sunday and the lay people another? Does the visiting team's assessment of what went on square with the congregation's or contradict it? Does what all these people say is happening on Sunday have any relationship to what the people in the congregation say a church ought to be? Does the event that these people talk about actually communicate the same view of the community that emerges from the rest of the data? So I established *coherence* as a principle and went back through the whole thing again to see which music programs contribute to coherence: which stand in the way of its emergence, and which are irrelevant.

Coherence in worship, in the sense used here, is not just the use on an individual Sunday of one theme or concept based on Scripture or what have you. I think that there is too much sole reliance on the lectionary to bring coherence to worship. People come to church seeking connections between their lives and the life in Christ. Being faced consistently with worship that is irrelevant to what they experience will sooner or later drive them away. Irrelevance is a form of incoherence, in the way I am using that term.

Coherence encompasses the tradition out of which a particular church comes as well as its self-understanding as a faith community in contemporary society. Coherence also encompasses the culture or cultures represented among the constituents of the church, such as the ethnic and regional patterns expressive of its identity. The rituals and aesthetic forms which manifest the inner life of these communities must express and nurture those qualities that permit the church to endure and thrive throughout the ages. Establishing the principle that worship be coherent is one way of measuring faithfulness.

But coherence is more than an interesting pattern emerging in a sociological study. Returning to the statement of one woman about her favorite hymn: worship on Sunday morning should be an event in which the way of following Christ is made alive among the community. Worship that is incoherent makes it very difficult for that "way" in all its facets and manifestations to come alive among a group of people. It also makes it difficult for a motley collection of people who gather in a room on Sunday to become a church focused on their ministry in the world.

Thus, when I speak of coherence, it is not only the coherence of ideas and concepts of good worship, but coherence of practice as well. Ideas become modified and transformed when they are incorporated into practice. If we extend the principle of coherence to include the practice of those who come to church, then church musicians must learn about the faith of the people who worship there and its coherent musical expression. Their work begins with the musical and religious culture of their particular congregation.

This coherence obtains not only in idea and method but also in practice. In this task, musicians and congregations are interdependent agents, since coherence between music and faith requires not only good leadership but also a congregation willing and able to participate in its musical life.

In churches where there existed a high degree of coherence in worship, the music programs had the following characteristics:

1. The musicians came from the same culture as the people in the congregation.
2. They were people of faith who understood the worship of their church from the inside out and the role of music in it.
3. They were good musicians, although their level of training varied widely.
4. They were able to work effectively with the resources at their disposal.
5. The building was conducive to music making and to the creation in worship of a feeling of communal presence.
6. The congregation was involved in the music making, both as participants (for example, good congregational singing) and as active listeners (for example, the choir had adequate resources to make the choir music come alive so that people could enter into the experience). This quality has everything to do with the choir director's abilities and his or her capacity to choose music within the reach of the people in the choirs.

Lack of coherence was attributable to many factors. I list the ones that either grew out of the music program or impinged on it in some way:

1. conflict among staff;
2. gulf of suspicion and lack of communication between staff and congregation;
3. lack of adequate training of musicians;
4. precarious existence of volunteer organizations, like the choirs, because of the lifestyle of the congregations;
5. conflicts growing out of pluralism of the congregation;
6. poor congregational singing.

Most of the items in these lists could fall under two headings: quality of the musical leadership and active cooperation between musicians and their congregations. If coherence between music and faith is to be achieved, then the congregation has to become active members in the work. Rather than sitting back on Sunday morning and expecting someone else to provide this coherence for them, they must come prepared to participate in the making of it. Musicians and other leaders of worship must undertake to train the congregation in music, to uncover its singing voice.

The musical activity of a congregation exemplifies the corporate nature of these religious practices that constitute worship. When a congregation hires a new music director, they ask someone to join the musical practices already established in the life of the congregation. These practices have forms, personnel, and repertories. They also carry the faith of the congregation. They may need rejuvenation, renovation, and deepening, but they are not the property of the music director or the pastor to change at will.

On the other hand, the various activities of corporate worship require practice for their mastery, and, in this day and age, we cannot assume that people who come to church know how to sing or pray. Some people have never been to church before. What do they make of these arcane activities? For others, Sunday morning is the only time they do many of the things worship requires of them. Until recently in the history of the church, Sunday worship was just one service in a pattern of worship which included daily family prayer and, in many traditions, several weekly meetings for singing and testifying. Corporate prayer consists of a series of religious practices which a congregation develops together. If a congregation does not sustain them, they will atrophy. For example, the singing tradition of the Methodists may simply die out unless congregations make the commitment to maintain it. In my travels to United Methodist churches, I found very little good congregational singing. The reason that the Mennonite four-part *a cappella* singing tradition still flourishes is that it is taught with care: families sing together at home during daily prayer, and children are trained in it at meeting on Sunday. And Episcopalians cannot take for granted that those who show up on Sunday are acquainted with the discipline of prayer implied in the forms in the Book of Common Prayer. Many people who are drawn to the Episcopal church come because of its distinctive worship, but do they understand what is required in its praying? Recently, several churches of the Reformed tradition have tried to reappropriate the systematic singing of the psalter with mixed results. "Ear-witness" accounts say that, during the Reformation, Geneva *rang* with the sound of those metrical psalms. What have we lost in neglecting this practice of our corporate past?

When Incoherent Worship Is Healthy

I would say that in some instances incoherence in worship in the project churches was a healthy sign rather than an unhealthy one. I don't think that a church can exist over a long period of time with incoherent worship, but I do think that healthy communities move in and out of it. It is the same way with conflict. A community can simply destroy itself in continuous fighting among members; yet conflict can also signal the emergence of new life. A period of incoherence in worship may ensue while a community gropes to find a way to express new insight into the life of faith. I was very interested in a comment a man made at a feedback session I led in one of the case-study churches. I described worshipping in his community that Sunday as frustrating because there was little opportunity for corporate response; there was a lot of music, but very few people seemed to know it and the organist, a substitute, didn't play it well. There was a lot of energy among individuals worshipping but no collective voice for it. He said, "You know, that's what we're trying to do in the other parts of our church lives. We're trying to find the voice of this particular congregation in this town, now, at this particular time."

Coherence is not the only principle by which one judges the integrity of the worship of a congregation. After all, the mass rallies of Hitler were very coherent events, and music played a big role in the expression of the "soul" of the Nazis. In order finally to claim that the worship of a particular church has integrity, one must return to the initial principle—the life of faith and its relationship to Faith. Theological norms must be established to measure the growth in faith of a community over several years. For the United Methodists in the project, these norms were derived from the Methodist Quadrilateral: Scripture, reason, tradition, and experience. For Episcopalians, adherence to the Book of Common Prayer was added to these more general theological claims.

Conclusion

A music program that contributes to the integrity of worship in a congregation will take on many guises. The musicians represented in the sample spanned a wide range. At one extreme was the person working in a small United Methodist church in the Berkshires who could not read music and who played everything by ear, but whose four member choir sang three anthems, with largely improvised harmony, the Sunday I arrived. At the opposite extreme was a nationally acclaimed organist and conductor who had ten paid soloists in his choir and who performed sections of the Verdi *Requiem* the Sunday I showed up there. In both instances, the music programs in their respective churches received very high marks from their congregations. Despite the distinctive quality of each program and the congregation's enthusiasm for them, the programs would fail if interchanged. The Verdi *Requiem* would be greeted with great politeness and enthusiasm in the church in the mountains, but for that congregation it would not be worship. Conversely the anthems of that tiny mountain choir would not be adequate to the worship life of the urban church. This music, too, would be greeted with politeness and enthusiasm, but soon people would want to expand the repertory to include other, more complex forms, beyond the scope of four people. Stating the point in these extremes focuses the issue clearly: good music programs take on the characteristics of the community of which they are an expression.

But the regulation of a good church music program does not end with coherence between it and the congregation's worship life. Two other issues are involved: the question of Faith with a capital F and the relationship between each choir and the congregation of which it is a part.

Issues of budget, organization, style, training, aesthetic standards, and personnel varied enormously from one congregation to the next. The constant among the myriad concrete examples of music programs in the project was the existence of faithful artists in active and supportive congregations. I have called these people artists to describe their capacity to work effectively with a sensuous object, like a hymn or responsorial psalm, but I do not mean to intimidate ordinary people by using this term. In my view, the "back-row bass," the professional organist, *and* the singing congregation are all artists, in that they are involved in the process of making these objects alive with their meaning.

In the next chapter, we will turn to the project data to see what they tell us about planning. All the good intentions and well-thought out programs will fail if the planning process in a church staff is faulty or inadequate.

CHAPTER 6

People Planning Worship

Introduction

In this chapter, we turn to a discussion of clergy and musicians planning for Sunday worship. Practicing the discipline of coherence between music and faith requires cooperation among the staff and between the staff and the congregation. Yet when the various planning structures are set up in a church, this type of interaction is often missing. What do the project data tell us about the way planning is currently done?

In several churches in the project, planning is accomplished efficiently and without major incident. In others it is a continuous source of tension. This weekly task has created major problems among many people over many years. How people work together can have an adverse effect on worship. Bad planning structures can in and of themselves create bad relationships among people, and bad relationships can make any structure useless no matter how carefully thought out. These behind-the-scene factors soon begin to show up on Sunday morning.

When I speak of planning structures, I mean both the explicit structures, like regularly scheduled staff meetings, and the implicit structures, like the unwritten patterns of "give and take" between two people. The explicit structures can be as elaborate as a chart of weekly meetings between clergy, musicians, and lay leaders from the congregation or as simple as a habitual conversation on the phone every other Wednesday afternoon. The implicit structures can also be either complex or simple––worked out over a period of years or established overnight in one long conversation. In the case study churches, most staffs employed a combination of explicit and implicit structures. To my knowledge, very few of them are subjected to regular evaluation.

What the data of the project suggest is that the issues of power—patterns of accountability and responsibility—and the lack of a shared understanding of worship among leaders and lay people in a congregation may lie behind much of the bad feeling between clergy and musicians. In our society with its therapeutic mind set, we tend to see relationships that are difficult as personality conflicts, and they can be that. But they also can be the product of badly managed or poorly thought out planning structures that distort or disrupt the capacity to accomplish tasks.

Institutional planning structures are explicit diagrams of the use of public power. The two denominations in this study differ in the way they think about planning for the use of music in worship. In the United Methodist *Book of Discipline* [1988], it is stated that responsibility for worship is primarily the pastor's, with consultation provided for through a chairperson of worship whose task it is to "cooperate with the pastor in planning and caring for worship, music and the other arts. . . . To the end that music and other arts may contribute largely to the communication and celebration of the gospel, the [worship] chairperson shall promote adequate musical leadership in the church." (Paragraph 261) In the project churches, a wide variety of planning structures obtained, as individual communities superimposed their own circumstances on this general rubric.

Episcopalians have a specific canon governing planning for worship:

> Canon 6. Sec. 1. It shall be the duty of every Minister to see that music is used as an offering for the glory of God and as a help to the people in their worship in accordance with the Book of Common Prayer and as authorized by the rubrics or by the General Convention of this Church. To this end the Minister shall have final authority in the administration of matters pertaining to music. In fulfilling this responsibility the Minister shall seek assistance from persons skilled in music. Together they shall see that music is appropriate to the context in which it is used.

It is clear that the priest has ultimate authority, but he or she is strongly encouraged to seek out musicians to help with the administration of music programs. How this relatively direct mandate for priestly authority worked itself out in the project churches was rarely clear. Like the United Methodists, local accommodation to the rubrics created many different patterns of authority and accountability.

In the following pages I will first of all compare the way clergy and musicians scored on the questionnaire, drawing conclusions about sources of agreement and disagreement between them. I will then turn to the case studies to look at successful and unsuccessful working structures and the relationships they fostered or hindered.

Results from the Questionnaire

Areas of Agreement

The data show remarkable agreement between clergy and musicians on a majority of the questions in the questionnaire. They agree on questions about mission, images and attributes of God, and patterns of church affiliation. There were only occasional differences on these issues. For example, clergy tend to score higher on issues of social justice. Musicians score higher on issues of patriotism.

One of the surprising areas of agreement is in musical training. The clergy in the sample showed strong interest and training in music!

39% consider themselves musicians;
45% are now or have been in the last five years members of an
    adult choir;
70% read music;
58% play instruments;
75% say they like to sing and do it well!

In addition, their scores on the question about the kind of music to be used in worship are similar. A majority of clergy and a plurality of musicians (63% and 41% respectively) agree that "any kind of music is appropriate as long as the congregation can use it to praise God." Their second choices (22% and 31% respectively) are also the same: "Since music in worship is an offering to God, only the best is appropriate."

When it comes to rating the music in their churches, clergy and musicians also agree. People were asked to assess the quality of Sunday worship. A majority of clergy and musicians (63% and 79% respectively) said the music program was generally satisfactory. The congregational singing got a less enthusiastic report from both groups. Only 41% of the clergy said the singing was satisfactory; 59% of the musicians said it was satisfactory.

So clergy and musicians share training and similar views about many aspects of their work together. Generally speaking, the clergy are more apt than musicians to think that change in the music program is called for; yet, there is not a wide gap between them. However, there are two areas of disagreement that show up in the data that point to possible problems. The first has to do with who should be in charge, and the second has to do with where the emphasis should be placed in the work to be done.

Areas of Disagreement

In the data musicians and clergy disagreed sharply on issues of authority. The figures that follow are, first, the sample taken as a whole and then the two denominations. Given the fact that Episcopalians are working under a canon which says that the clergy have control over the music program and that United Methodists mandate some form of lay participation in planning, it is interesting to see how their scores compare to the rubrics. People were asked to voice agreement or disagreement on the following statement about who was in charge of the music program: "A committee consisting of staff and lay leaders should have control over the music program in the church."

Fifty-six per cent of the clergy *agreed*, 18% of them strongly, and 61% of the musicians *disagreed*, 50% of them strongly. Looking at the scores by denomination: For Episcopalians, 62% of the clergy *disagreed*, 31% of them strongly; 64% of the musicians *disagreed*, all of them strongly. For United Methodists, 83% of the clergy *agreed*, 33% of them strongly; and 58% of the musicians *disagreed*, 41% of them strongly.

Although a majority of Episcopal clergy and musicians are in agreement that a committee of lay people and staff *should not* have control of the music program, they disagree about who should choose the hymns. Asked if the director of music should choose the hymns, 75% of the clergy *disagreed*, 13% of them strongly; and 58% of the musicians *agreed*, 33% of them strongly. Despite the mandate of the *Book of Discipline* about lay responsibility for worship, United Methodist musicians *do not* think that a committee of lay and staff leaders should have control over the music in the church!

Checking the scores of the congregations on the question of who should have control over the music program, the data are split 50/50 between the two options.

In the sample, musicians were, by and large, the people who made the ordinary, everyday decisions about music in worship, excluding perhaps choosing the hymns. They were the ones with the "on site" responsibility. But the data suggest that their authority to make decisions that ultimately affect the worship life of their congregations is not necessarily granted by either their clergy sisters and brothers or by the congregation. The responses to these particular statements in the questionnaire show that there is sharp disagreement about where the locus of power should be.

Another important area of disagreement between clergy and musicians cropped up in response to a question about the most meaningful musical activity during worship. Seventy-nine per cent of the clergy and 38% of the musicians rank hymns as the most meaningful; 7% of the clergy and 41% of the musicians rank anthems as the most meaningful. These data may reveal a difference about the focus of musical resources in the church. Musicians spend many more hours thinking about and practicing anthems and preludes and postludes than they do hymns. Is there a disagreement between clergy and musicians about what kind of work a musician should be doing during the week?

Since many musicians work without contracts and job descrip-tions, they are often hampered by unclear and unspoken expectations and blurry lines of accountability. Having to make so many decisions that affect the worship life of a community in a situation where power is exercised in an ambiguous manner can lead to great hesitancy and frustration. Moreover, feelings of isolation and bewilderment can result from working in institutions, such as congregations, in which parishioners do not see what goes on behind the scenes during the week but do exert considerable influence over what one does on Sunday morning. In this, they are like many of their clergy brothers and sisters who have ample authority but find it difficult to effect change in the church where the congregation, collectively and through its representatives, exerts so much power.

Planning That Works: Church A

We turn now to the case studies of two churches to see how planning
actually takes place, how successful it is, and how each of these churches
solves the problems that the data uncovered.

The most unusual, colorful, and complex planning structure
existed in Church A. Here is a description of their planning process
taken from staff interviews.

> The parish secretary prays for the bulletin. We have a staff meet-
> ing each week, and we know if there's a guest or a special theme,
> and she takes two or three mornings of prayer, herself, what the
> scripture [is], the prayer of confession . . . or maybe there's some
> special little thing happening, so . . . that is part of her ministry: to
> take time for prayer and to hear from the Lord, and put in the pray-
> er of confession and the scripture that *God* has for that week.

> The organist independently prays and hears from the Lord
> as to what hymns and special music she's to play. The Music
> Ministry does the same. They are in prayer and the Music Day,
> Saturday, they have prayer and fasting that day. They spend an
> hour of prayer and preparation and sharing and scripture reading
> before they even go to do the "praise and worship" section. The
> dancers, the same. They're independently praying and fasting and
> interceding for the church [asking] "What is the Spirit saying,
> what is the Spirit directing for that Sunday?" The same with the
> lay reader. . . .The lay reader prays and fasts for what direction
> would God have in terms of the life of the service and the same
> with the preacher. Everybody is totally, totally independent.

> And it comes together with a power and with a dynamism
> that is awesome. It's refreshing every Sunday, it's awesome to
> me as pastor to see what the Lord has said to the lay reader, to see
> what the Lord has said to the dancers, to the musicians, to the or-
> ganist, to the ushers and greeters who may have a special word or
> a prayer of blessing as everybody's coming in.

When asked about planning, the organist had the following to say:

> Before, the pastor or minister would tell me what hymns would go

with his sermons or whatever; but in this case I was told [to
choose the hymns] and I went along with it, and so then I said,
"I definitely have to pray because I don't know what he's preaching [about], and I haven't got the time or it's very difficult to get
to him and sometimes he might change—the Lord might change—
his sermon at the last minute. So I have to! There's only one person that knows that, so I always seek His [God's] help! He usually
gives me maybe a one word—Love would be the theme for this
Sunday—and I would start choosing hymns, and I would play
them from the hymnal, and I would know from in my spirit if that
was really the hymn because I'd have peace, I'd be able to play it
very well.

Further along in the interview the organist made this comment about
worship planning in the church:

Well, in years past there was joint planning, as you say. But I
think that because our congregation has come to the point of being
able to praise and worship with a team, I don't think that we really
have to work together that closely, I mean we pray and we—well,
I don't mean that we *don't* have to meet together, we do work together . . . . I don't think that we have to really plan that because I
don't think *we're* the planners. You know? The Holy Spirit [is
the planner].

Worship on Sunday in this church is a mixture of spontaneous and
pre-arranged segments. The style is very informal; there is considerable
interchange between those leading worship and the people in the pews.
Things begin and end when they need to. The pastor has some responsibility for the movement of worship from one thing to another and occasionally has to exercise restraint when someone goes on too long or
things get bogged down. In the group interview there was an exchange
between the pastor and the leader of the Music Ministry about who had
ultimate control. They agreed that the pastor had the authority to control
the music in worship but rarely exercised it. They had developed a set of
hand signals to communicate to one another about the way the service
moved.

Here there are no constraints about time. Things begin at the stated
time and end when they end. The pastor admitted that occasionally the

service seemed flat and lifeless. That usually happened when they were trying too hard or had prepared too long and too carefully. Normally, however, there is quite a lot of energy and enthusiasm in the room, coming from people in leadership positions and in the pews. People have learned to relax and rely on the Spirit to take their efforts and reshape them to create the whole.

This informal, multi-layered planning structure rests on a shared view of the nature of the work people are doing and how it fits together on Sunday. Although the service has a lot of room to "give" as the Spirit moves, it has an order or logic to it that rarely changes. Everyone knows the order and knows their role in it. The structure also grows out of an explicit "life style" that everyone shares. What they do is based in prayer and fasting, and everyone—leaders and other members of the congregation—participates in it. It is cohesive from the start. The leader of the Music Ministry had this to say about preparation for worship:

> Worship will only be as good on a Sunday morning as what they've been doing all week individually. In other words, if you've been in the world and running wild with all the things in the world and not being the Christian you're supposed to be, and then you pop in on Sunday morning, thinking "Just touch God and he's going to touch you." And half an hour, like during the music—and I'm talking just the music—it's like "No way!" because what happened is. . . . And I've seen it in my life, you know, I've had both sides of the fence, so maybe that's an advantage; where I haven't been living the way I should have been living. And then I go to church Sunday thinking I'm going to worship God and touch Him and He's going to touch me. Twenty minutes I spend trying to shake off guilt, feelings of hypocrisy, feelings of, like, condemnation. Then I may have ten minutes left where maybe I'll experience God. So people will experience, people will worship only to the same degree that they're living it every day. And we're lucky. This is a church where people are real about it for the most part; you can walk in their house any time of day or night and probably live in it the way they would appear on Sunday morning. That's like a gift. But if we had a congregation where it was just Sunday morning Christians worshipping—awful!

This complex planning structure worked amazingly well. It was of a piece with the values and intentions of the particular congregation. In the pastor it had a person who could work comfortably with a team of people and "go with the flow" on Sunday morning. This particular community was not without its tensions. However they did not adversely affect preparation for worship.

Planning That Doesn't Work: Church B

The various groups responsible for worship on Sunday in Church A worked together with little friction. In many churches this was not the case. The research teams found tension between clergy and musicians to be common. Some of it was dealt with directly; some of it was acknowledged and not dealt with; some of it was unacknowledged. We turn now to one case where the relationship between the pastor and the musicians led to chaos on Sunday morning.

In Church B worship on Sunday suffered because of a conflict between the musicians on the staff and the pastor. This conflict is exemplified in the pastor's practice of leading the hymn singing and the organist's way of undermining it. In the following exchanges during the various interviews, the source of this conflict emerges.

In the interview with the pastor, the question of the vitality of the congregational singing came up. Here is what he said:

> Oh yes, it sure does [have vitality]. But I must say, in all modesty, that it's because of my singing by and large because I lead the congregation into singing of the hymns. You sing out lustfully and cheerfully and joyfully and articulately. When I lead worship, I worship. In other words, I'm not a professional up there as such leading the congregation in worship. I'm worshipping, too. And I really get into that at times, and sometimes I lose myself, and it's no problem, you know, there's nothing wrong with that. And there are people who say that when I'm not present, they really miss that. They really miss the singing.

In an interview with the music director, the interviewer mentioned that the pastor considered it his responsibility to lead the singing. The musician responded:

That is a traditional perspective that should no longer be held. In the
setting where you have a hundred and fifty or two hundred people
worshipping, and you have a choir and an organ, then the choir and
the organ are to be the medium of leadership, the pastor is not. I
think that it is an inappropriate perspective that is disruptive. It is
disruptive to the choir, it is disruptive to me because what I do is
generally put close to full organ on and just go my own way and
push. And that is the best I can do. Normally the message gets
across by the end of the first verse, and you are either going to follow me, or we are going to have trouble. And I don't like to be like
that—you know, muscle my way through something like that. But
that seems to be the way—again, it's stomping your feet and saying,
"Listen up, would you please?" You know—"Either that, or do it by
yourself." Otherwise, there is no leadership. I mean, it's splintered.
It's all over the place.

In speaking to the pastor and to the musicians, very different stories about the planning process for worship on Sunday also came out.
The interviewer asked one of the musicians about how planning takes
place:

I do mine, and he does his. I try to maintain a sense of season, for
one thing. Working liturgically, on a liturgical basis. But his perspective is that people are really not interested in that kind of thing.
All they want to do is come and hear a good sermon. Why one has
to be exclusive of the other, I've never quite understood. Worship
suffers because of it. I think he . . . feels that, you know, it's up to
me to kind of keep that [liturgical] undercurrent going. If I don't it's
fine, too, no problem here. And if I do, it just answers the needs of
some people, and it takes another burden off of him. That's it, no
worry. "I can trust you." And that's all. It simplifies things for
him. I would like to see a different perspective.

The pastor, on the other hand, had this to say about the planning
process:

Well, the person that preaches here orders the worship service and
picks out the hymns; the hymns, the themes to go with the sermon,
primarily, to give unity to the total worship experience. Stan and

JoAnne [the names have been changed throughout these reports]
know what our sermon themes are going to be ahead of time. Then
they work the anthems into that as best they can. We have a staff
meeting about once every three weeks, but I see Stan almost three or
four times a week. And we have a very good relationship with each
other, fortunately. And Mason [JoAnne's last name]—terrific person. Very capable and very cooperative, and so we really don't have
any difficulty. We try to work with each other and work around
when we're going to have special music on special days and when
the choir's going to have a Sunday, and when the Youth Choir's
going to present their, whatever they present. And it isn't easy because we have so much going on here. Sometimes we're just step-
ping on top of each other. And so we have to work closely together
to be able to do all that and coordinate it.

Here we have a situation in which the principals are not really
talking to one another. In the past, attempts were made to bridge the gulf
between the two sides, but for some reason they were unsuccessful. The
result was that the pastor's habits and views held sway but were under-
mined by the musician at the organ on Sundays. The pastor was unaware
that a major problem existed; the musicians were demoralized and angry.

The divergence in descriptions of worship, the planning process,
and the nature of the relationships among these people also showed up in
the various views of the Sunday morning the research team attended
worship. Reading the myriad reports of the event, I found it hard to de-
cipher what actually was going on because there were so many conflict-
ing views of it. Clergy and musicians had very different stories to tell
about what went on that particular Sunday, and what the research team
reported differed in many ways from the reported experience of the
leaders of worship and representatives from the congregation. All the
people in leadership positions in this church had talent and training, and
they worked very hard, but the effect of the lack of real contact among
them was to turn all of their efforts into chaos on Sunday.

Several problems in this church needed to be addressed. Personality
conflicts were definitely going on. But there also was no shared understanding of what the nature of worship in that community was, or of
who was in charge of what on Sunday. The musicians were given responsibilities, but the situation under which they had to operate did not
provide them with the authority to make changes they felt were important.

The pastor remained isolated from them, functioning without any real idea of the resentment and anger of his colleagues. Because the pastor's public authority in the church always overrode the musicians', the musicians had to resort to "private" machinations to achieve their goals. This led to a distortion of power as evidenced in the battle about the hymn singing on Sunday.

Conclusion

Clearly planning raises issues of accountability and the nature of leadership. What can be learned from looking at the planning structures of these two churches? First of all, Church A had a structure that grew out of its common life; that is to say, the way planning was done for worship on Sunday was congruent with the values and intentions of the community. Second, although there was a lot of team effort involved in which many people were given areas of responsibility, on Sunday two "persons" were in charge. The pastor had penultimate authority and the Holy Spirit had ultimate authority. And everyone, leadership and congregation alike, agreed to this scheme. Third, the people who had responsibility for a segment of worship had the authority to make decisions. They were not working in a structure that asked them to think about what they were doing and then at the last minute go along with someone else's ideas, thereby wasting what they had spent time and effort doing. Responsibility, accountability, and the power to act resided in each of these groups. Yet, if the Spirit chose to alter the plans, everyone gave in to it. Fourth, the pastor could work effectively in the midst of what seemed like chaos. He definitely found working in this style to be invigorating. And last, and most important, the structure was undergirded by prayer on the part of everyone—leadership and congregation alike. People came to worship on Sunday prepared. In this church, the planning, although very elaborate, accomplished its goals. Methods were congruent with the nature of the community.

In Church B, none of these things obtained. Pastor and musicians had two very different views of the nature of leadership. The responsibility for the music was thwarted by the possibility that all the thought and work would be overturned without consultation. Little if any communication was going on among the people responsible for worship and between the leaders of worship and the congregation. Therefore all lines of accountability and authority for both pastor and musicians were blurred; those functioning seemed to be arbitrary and quixotic. The result was chaos on Sunday morning.

Church B is an extreme instance of a common problem. Personal animosity was rife in the staff. Are there solutions? In brief, I would advocate prayer on the part of all concerned as the first and constant task. Second, I would initiate conversation about authority and the purposes of worship among people in leadership and representatives of the congregation. This conversation would later involve the whole congregation, perhaps beginning with an adult education program. Third, the same persons should create (or review and, if necessary, revise) a statement of the purposes of worship and of explicit structures of accountability and evaluation, for both clergy and musicians.

CHAPTER 7

Choosing Music for Worship

Introduction

There is an assumption running through the various chapters of this book
that I wish to make explicit here and then discuss. A congregation needs
adequate musical resources in order that the connection between its faith
and music live and grow. Sounds simple, doesn't it! But it isn't. When
categories of adequacy and inadequacy come into play, we are speaking
about making judgments. Judgments imply standards. Standards are
multi-faceted and complex; they vary according to musical traditions; but
they exist, and people need to pay attention to them.

    In the Introduction to the book, I asked a question that is related to
musical standards: Does the music program have integrity within the
context of the religious tradition of the congregation? I have discussed at
length the church musician's responsibility to the congregation and its
religious traditions. The very nature of music entails a level of responsiveness from the singers or listeners. If the music used in worship is
consistently irrelevant to the congregation, it will be ignored. Each congregation has its own culture, the Incarnation appears among people in
many guises, and judgments about the musical repertory of a community
are not made easily. Any set of worship and music practices developed
in one community cannot be imposed with impunity on another because
these practices may do violence to that community's religious identity.
To complicate matters further, congregations are not culturally homogeneous. Each displays many musical vocabularies.

    But a musician's purpose in the worship life of a congregation is
not simply to supply music that is familiar, that operates within the
parameters of a congregation's musical vocabulary. A steady diet of the

"tried-and-true" is inadequate for many reasons. Just as the preacher has a teaching role in the community, so does the musician. So making choices about music is unavoidable. How are they made and who makes them?

In my experience, the bitterest conflicts about choosing music that surface among musicians, pastors, and congregations today revolve around popular music. People involved in these arguments are often confusing two very different issues: the quality of the music and its style. They lump the two together, as, for example, when they blanketly condemn a particular style of music, like gospel music, as lacking any aesthetic value. I want to separate them and examine each issue in turn. These are very old arguments. The history of church music is littered with these polemics. A student of American church history can read Thomas Hastings on the demise of psalmody in the wake of the religious renewal of the 1830s in upstate New York, and then turn to Horatio Parker's acerbic condemnation of Ira D. Sankey's music in the urban revivals of the 1880s and 1890s in England and the United States. However, these issues need to be addressed in their contemporary manifestations because they still generate conflict. I will begin by setting forth an explanation of the nature of aesthetic judgments and then turn to the question of style.

Aesthetic Judgments

Let us return to a statement made by a member of the staff of the church referred to in the Introduction.

> Part of our job is to do the best we can in ways that give our best understandings of ourselves and of the nature of the liturgy and of the congregation, to build over time a liturgy that embodies both the truth of what we're doing and the life of the congregation.

What we are doing as worshipping people and as leaders of worshipping people is to "build over time a liturgy that embodies . . . the truth of what we're doing and the life of the congregation . . . ." What this person implies is that there are standards of truth brought into play in the evaluation of what we do as singers, worshippers, and planners. In other words, any old thing will not do! What is entailed in this truth telling?

Charles Morgan, an English drama critic, explains the function of dramatic art in terms that point out its importance to us:

"Dramatic art has . . . a double function—first to still the preoccupied mind, to empty it of triviality, to make it receptive and meditative; then to impregnate it" [1933:70].

Elsewhere in the article, he describes this process in more detail:

The order of [this] experience is always the same—a shock, and after the shock, an inward stillness, and from that stillness an influence emerging, which transmutes him. Transmutes *him*—not his opinions. . . . It is the enveloping movement of the whole drama upon the soul of man. We surrender and are changed" [1933:64].

I quote a drama critic here because his words echo the sentiments of many parishioners when they talked about the effect of music in worship. Along with gathering people together and moving the liturgy along, music "empties the mind of triviality, makes it receptive and then impregnates it." In this process, "we surrender and are changed."

The question is, "With what are worshippers being impregnated?" Is this music worth anything? In seeking to answer this question, we are making aesthetic judgments. A further question is, "Is the way the music is performed adequate to its potential for transformation?" Are we doing it well? In asking this question, we are evaluating the resources necessary to bring to life the hymns and anthems used in worship, resources which include the congregation. Music is a powerful teacher of the life of faith. It takes up a lot of time in worship. If it is corrupt, badly done, or trivial, worship suffers.

What is entailed in aesthetic judgments? Again we are faced with arguments that fill library shelves with answers. Here I want to give a clear, succinct explanation, based on a discussion in Susanne Langer's *Feeling and Form* [1953:380f]. I will set out several characterizations, featuring Langer's view of art as "envisagement of feeling":

1. The art work is a well-constructed envisagement of true feeling.
2. It is a badly constructed envisagement of true feeling. Langer

calls this category "poor" art: It is true but misses the mark as craft. It is an instance of the artist struggling to master the techniques that would express something genuine about human experience. It can also be a congregation struggling to sing an unfamiliar hymn or a small choir singing an anthem that is much too difficult for them.

3. It is a well-constructed envisagement of corrupted feeling. In my view, this is the only really pernicious type of music—music that *lies effectively* about human experience.

4. It is something altogether different, like a copy of someone else's ideas or an envisagement of what people ought to be feeling. This, in Langer's view, is non-art.

In this view, aesthetic judgments entail judgments about candor—how true to life the art work is—and about craft—how well the art work is done or performed.

Making Judgments about Music

The responsibility of those planning worship is, to the best of their abilities given the resources at hand, to "build over time a liturgy that embodies *both* the truth of what we're doing and the life of the congregation." [Italics mine.] One of the great mistakes musicians and worship leaders often make is to think that judgments solely on the aesthetic merits of music are adequate. In worship, aesthetic judgments come laden with theological and liturgical considerations. Let's return for a moment to the musician's reactions quoted in the Introduction. Here I reproduce his statement in its entirety.

Well, I've been in this racket long enough to know that I certainly cannot depend upon others. For one thing, in church music, since there's no applause—and applause is a bad gauge anyhow—you don't get feedback. What feedback you do get from others is liable to be special pleading—it's liable to be "I like that!" and what that's liable to mean is "It reminds me of an anthem we used to sing in St. Swithin's in the Swamp forty years ago." Or when it's negative, that's liable to mean, "We never did anything like that at Saint

Swithin's in the Swamp." It's very rarely based upon anything either musical or spiritual that is in fact appropriate to the circumstances here at St. Thomas. . . . That probably sounds pretty stuffy—
—I mean it strikes me that what I'm really saying is that I'll decide whether it's good or bad, thank you very much. But it—in some sense, I think that's what any musician has to do.

This church musician is complaining about two things: the lack of adequate feedback on his work and the poor musical and spiritual judgment of the congregation. Having come to these conclusions, he then decides that, since others are undependable, he is forced to make aesthetic judgments on his own.

His clergy friends temper his arguments somewhat by both agreeing and disagreeing with him. One says that the fact that music in worship may have echoes of the past may not be a bad thing, since rituals depend on these echoes for part of their power and importance.

Well, I don't know. Your comment about verbal response and what that frequently will mean—whether it's positive or negative—brings to mind a workshop that I went to with [a wel-known liturgical scholar]. He was talking about ritual, and—I guess I'm questioning based on what he said about ritual and what that does for people—I'm questioning whether the fact that [the music] *does* remind me of what we used to do in St. Swithin's in the Swamp is all bad . . . because, as [this scholar] says, the purpose of ritual is to recreate, to bring back a moment, if you will, or a piety.

Another counters by saying that the desire for the familiar may block people from judging the unfamiliar. If the criteria for judgment are derived only from the known, then they are woefully inadequate.

What I heard Sam saying was not so much that it's bad to be back at St.—you know, to have those echoes—but that you can't judge the quality of what you do, the value of what you do, by the response of people who, because they didn't do that kind [of thing at] St. Swithin's, don't know how to respond to the music *here*. . . .

Looking closely at these comments, one recognizes that the judgments that the "St. Swithin's" people are making are not basically aesthetic, but liturgical. In the reported criticism about the music, they are saying, "The music of worship needs to provide a voice for my faith." This judgment may have nothing to do with aesthetic standards.

Making aesthetic judgments based on our own musical understanding is not adequate because what has candor to us may not appear that way to people in the congregation. We have to learn how to make these judgments for groups of people whose life of faith is as wide-ranging as their musical tastes. Our task is to find, or write, good music that is expressive of the life of faith of the congregation. To do so means learning about the musical and faith lives of the people in the pews. Fortunately, the two go together: Learning the music of people *is* learning their faith. Musician and congregation join in a mutual education project, in which a variety of musical expressions are shared among people of different ages, cultures, and traditions.

Having made the point about mutual responsibility, I do believe that the decisions about the music in worship are best made by musicians, here defined as people who have spent their lives developing their responsiveness to musical symbols. That pastors are frequently endowed with musical talent and training is certainly a plus here. There are disciplines involved in making these decisions, and, for the church musician, these are both musical and theological in content. They are not easily made and, therefore, should not be haphazardly made.

Practically speaking, I would get the "St. Swithin's" people to sit down and tell me *why* music there was so powerful. What communicated their faith so effectively? I would ask them what, given the resources available to us in this congregation, could be done now. I would explain how I see my work among them and talk to them about the range of musical vocabularies and traditions in the congregation and in the history of the church. In other words, I would use the opportunity to *learn* about the *faith* of the people entrusted to my care but also to *teach* them about the *broader musical tradition*. In short, I would become a music educator as my own faith is broadened and deepened.

Musical Style

We turn now to a discussion about the nature of musical style. In one of the Episcopal case-study churches, I interviewed a man who wanted to change the prevailing style of music in his church. This man had great affection and respect for the musicians of the church but wanted to expand the repertory of the music program. At the time of the project, the entire staff, including musicians, ministers, and lay leaders, had been dealing unsuccessfully with a vocal segment of the congregation who were complaining about the formal style of the music program. Although the research team did not spend a long enough time in the parish to draw anything but tentative conclusions about this conflict, it was their impression that wrangling about musical style was a surface manifestation of a deeper theological conflict. This is often the case in congregations. The music program is a lightning rod for general discontent.

What is style? In general usage, style means the form or manner of a thing as opposed to its content or subject matter. One might say of a speech: "She gave that speech in a very concise style!" meaning that the form in which she delivered her ideas was clear and to the point. Yet in the discussion of style in the new *Grove's Dictionary of Music* the distinctions between form or manner and content are not so neatly drawn. *Grove's* defines style as "manner, mode of expression, type of presentation. . ." and then says, " [T]o treat of the style of an epoch or culture, one is treating of import, a substantive communication from a society, which is a significant embodiment of the aspirations and inner life of its people." The manner of presentation of an idea communicates something of substance. According to A. C. Kroebel in *Style and Civilizations*, the ingredients of style in art consist in 1) the subject matter chosen, 2) the "'concept' of the subject, along with its emotional aura. . ." and 3) the specific, technical form given in execution of the work [1957: 30]. What is of interest to a particular composer or painter, how she or he conceives of the subject and how its emotional valence is projected, and finally the means or medium of that projection all communicate "the aspirations and inner life" of a culture.

In music, style is a very important aspect of its meaning. Think for a minute of the contrast between a congregation in a predominantly white suburb and a congregation in a predominantly black urban neighborhood singing the spiritual "Let my people go." Ostensibly the subject matter is the same in both instances, yet the style of singing so changes what is sung that the two "singings" have divergent meanings. The contrast in style comes mainly from two interrelated factors: 1) the difference in the relationship between the text and the inner lives of the singers and 2) the singing traditions of the two communities.

In the case of the relationship between the text and the lives of the singers, the experience that African-Americans bring to the singing of the hymn is very different from that of people of the dominant culture. Oppression is a pervasive reality to African-Americans; the singing of that spiritual is a rallying cry that comes deep from their souls. Whites in a suburb might empathize with their sisters and brothers in the black neighborhood, but they will not sing the song with the same immediacy and conviction.

In the case of the singing traditions of the two communities, the immediacy of the cry "Let my people go" is reinforced by the past legacy of those communities who trace their ancestry back to the slave quarters that gave birth to the spirituals. That past, handed down in the improvisational quality of singing that evokes the drum in its rhythms and melodic complexity, is reappropriated by every generation in the style of their singing. This singing tradition shapes the event by linking the faith and endurance of the slave to the contemporary African-American confronting the racism of the dominant culture. The people in the white church do not have this legacy to inform their singing. Their singing does not have the echoes of the drum in it. (Indeed, until recently, this musical tradition was virtually ignored by editors of their hymnals, an omission that betrayed our society's racist judgments about musical value.) They sing this spiritual with the echoes of their own Euro-American traditions in it. Thus the styles of the two renditions of the same text shape the very core of the meaning of the experience.

Conflicting Musical Styles

What might be involved in the conflict about musical styles? As part of my analysis of the project data, I grouped people by their favorite hymns and studied their answers to the questionnaire. For instance, among those choosing the hymn "Amazing Grace," I found many similarities between Episcopalians and United Methodists, and between those United Methodists for whom "Amazing Grace" was their favorite hymn and all other United Methodists. But when I compared Episcopalians for whom "Amazing Grace" is their favorite hymn with all other Episcopalians, the discrepancies began to surface. One of the most significant was the percentage of people raised in the denomination: among "Amazing Grace" people only 16 percent of them were raised Episcopalians as compared to 47 percent of all other Episcopalians in the sample.

Other differences grew out of their adherence to more evangelical forms of piety and belief, many of which are congruent with the images of the hymn but incongruent with the more formal style of public worship in most present-day New England Episcopal churches. First, in their view of the church and its mission to the world, the "Amazing Grace" Episcopalians differ significantly from their denominational counterparts in three categories. In two categories they consider the activities mentioned to be *more* important to the mission of the church than their denominational counterparts: a) "Opening members' hearts and minds to the spiritual gifts of miracles, and healing, and to the baptism of the Holy Spirit;" b) "Preparing church members for a world to come in which the cares of this world are absent." In a third category they consider the activities to be *much less* important: c) "Encouraging church members to reach their own decisions on issues of faith and morals even if this diminishes the church's ability to speak with a single voice on these issues."

Second, their religious experience is centered in the intimacy of a small group. They are more likely to meet for prayer and Bible study and to discuss religious beliefs with others, to image God as a close companion and emphasize God as presence rather than a symbol or idea. They are likely to go on retreats and to have powerful spiritual experiences more frequently than their denominational counterparts.

Third, their affiliation with the people in their congregation is more significant to them. More of them are very attached to their church, consider their communities more closely knit, and would be very upset if they had to leave them.

These findings suggest that "Amazing Grace" embodies for these Episcopalians a variety of religious experience epitomized by the small prayer group and characterized by intense personal experience of God and the building of strong bonds of affection and intimacy among its members. Because of its images and melody and also its informality of style—the fact that people know it by heart and can sing it anywhere—"Amazing Grace" provides a vehicle for the expression of the ethos of these small groups within a congregation. Still it would have seemed out of place on Sunday morning intermixed with the more austere and objective language cadences of the Book of Common Prayer.

Returning to the church whose staff meeting I quoted at length, a group of people in this particular church were trying to make changes in the Sunday liturgy through the introduction of less formal types of music.

But from my analysis of "Amazing Grace" Episcopalians, I conclude that they were also trying to give public voice to powerful aspects of their religious experience, to change the nature of the gathering of the community, and thereby change the nature of the community. What appeared to be a conflict about hymns like "Amazing Grace" really was a controversy about the nature of the Christian community.

In seeking a change in the prevailing musical style, the man referred to above (page 71) posed a very complex challenge for his community. He himself was not raised an Episcopalian, but found himself attracted to its highly symbolic worship practices. He was very attached to this church, yet found its formal style of worship limiting. He and many others like him were challenging many of the prevailing religious traditions of the community through an argument about music.

The Importance of the Tradition

Returning for a moment to the example of "Let My People Go," we saw there the importance of a musical tradition to the faith of a community. The loss of the improvisatory style of singing among African-Americans would mean the loss of an important aspect of their identity. Although largely unnoticed, the past and its traditions are brought to worship every Sunday in the memories of the congregation. They reside in the buildings, patterns of gathering, and especially in the forms of worship that have endured over time. The present is often so compelling an experience that it masks the presence of the past. However, in the face of change, the past intrudes forcibly into the present. It can take over the present.

Recall for a moment the discussion of "mythos" in Chapter 1 [see above, page 8]. Traditions are important (and powerful) because they are saturated with what Bernard Meland would call a community's *mythos.* "Mythos" encompasses and fashions the expressive forms which *tell* the identity of a community and of its faith. These forms are myths and stories, images and symbols, events and rituals. Meland is speaking here of a level of experience, often subconscious, that precedes and supports what we would recognize as ordinary experience—the sensibilities that declare what is valued, what is cherished, what is intended by a community.

The formal and somewhat introverted style of worship at that

Episcopal church carried many things of value to that community. By challenging the style, the critics were challenging the very nature of the community. Communities do not take lightly a threat to the symbol system undergirding the meaning of their lives. This goes for musicians, too. Today, numbers of musicians are finding their life's work dismissed out-of-hand by their congregations. They experience it as not only a portent of economic hardship but also a threat to their very existence because their system of meaning is lost.

In its recent past, this particular congregation had suffered a major disruption—a move from one building to another. In an interview, one of the staff members expressed some reservations about this move from the smaller, more intimate space into the larger, more municipal-looking one:

> Why did a congregation that was in a warm, small, self–enclosed, Yankee Gothic Episcopal church—why did they build this building? Because they went from a room that was "womby" and enclosing and warm and all those things that you think of a nice, dark room—a little Yankee Episcopal church at its best—and then came over here and built a congregational preaching building with a chancel tacked on to it, with big, clear glass windows that invite the world in, and the absolute, architecturally and emotionally, absolute antithesis of where they'd been.

This person recognizes this move as the source of a deep fissure in the collective memory of the congregation and wonders to what extent it still influences the behavior of the people gathering there today.

Negotiating the Conflict between Styles

I have used these examples to illustrate the importance to the religious lives of people in a congregation of its style of music. Each community will have to negotiate the conflict between innovation and tradition in its own way. In the particular church discussed, shortly after the project team visited the church, the music director resigned. His successor was chosen because of her ability to work in many different styles of music. In another church, the early service was informal and the later one more formal. In yet another, a small lay committee responsible for worship

spent several years coming to their particular brand of compromise.
Here is the rector speaking about it.

> That group [endured] most of the blood, sweat, and tears because
> most of the conflict about renewal here all focused in on the wor-
> ship. To the point where one year the conflict got so bad that we
> split the liturgy up. So we had a more traditional liturgy at 9 and a
> more charismatic liturgy—folk—guitars—at 11. In principle, I was
> really opposed to that, but there was such a lack of charity in the
> community—factions—that whenever we sang praise songs, the
> more traditional element would sort of snarl, and more, laugh. . . .
> They sort of mocked the charismatics raising their hands. The cha-
> rismatic wing, if we sang a canticle or something more traditional, a
> lot of them would say, "Oh, we're squelching the Spirit!" I remem-
> ber one woman came and told me, "God told me . . . He wants to get
> rid of all the prayer books. They're an abomination to Him." Any-
> way, we finally split the service, but I told the congregation it was
> for our hardness of heart. This was not a political compromise to
> make everyone happy. This was a public confession of our sin, that
> we are a divided parish, that we don't love each other enough that
> we can't even worship together. But out of that whole year came a
> spirit of repentance because it was at the end of that year that we
> came back together into the formal liturgy that we still have now
> where that conflict really dissipated.

Whatever the outcome of such controversies, resolving rather than
suppressing them is essential to the continuing health of a community.
In this day and age, a musician cannot count on presiding over a music
program for a congregation whose musical vocabularies are of one style
or genre. In most congregations, fewer than half of the people there on a
Sunday morning were raised in that denomination or religious tradition.
Some have never been to church before. With many other religious or
quasi-religious organizations (such as Al Anon, Compassionate Friends,
and other self-help groups) thriving in our society, the church no longer
has hegemony, if it ever did, over the religious culture of a particular
congregation.

Conclusion

If the society, in the face of all of these recent budget cuts, is becoming increasingly musically illiterate, the church will have to take over the role of music educator. Music is vital to the life of faith. We cannot assume that people know how to sing or that a congregation knows how to use the various forms, like hymns, anthems, and responses, to express and form their faith. Forming multiple choirs, teaching singing to the children, having hymn sings, Pops concerts, and Sing-spirations—in short, finding ways to get people involved in music making— will further this education process.

ENDNOTES

Kroebel, A. L. *Style and Civilizations*. Westport, Conn.: Greenword Press, 1957.

Langer, Susanne. *Feeling and Form*. New York: Scribner, 1953.

Morgan, Charles. "The nature of dramatic illusion," *Essay by Divers Hands: being the Transactions of the Royal Society of Literature of the United Kingdom*. N.S. V. XII, ed. by R.W. Macan. London: Oxford University Press, 1933.

CHAPTER 8

Conclusion

The Music in Churches Project involved hundreds of people who were concerned, in one way or another, with the music making in their churches. They were busy providing a musical voice for faith. What I uncovered in the project was the complex and multi-faceted quality of this practice of church music. It resembles a motley, in the original sense of that word, "exhibiting a great diversity of elements and of different differing sounds, differing modes of performance, differing repertories. If this variety obtained in a small geographical area, among people whose origins were mainly English, imagine what would obtain when extended to areas where English is one among many languages, where Puritan culture does not predominate?

My understanding of this rather ordinary musical practice found in churches has changed a great deal in the last several years. In the process of doing the project, I began to think of church music in broader terms to make room for its variety; I also began to let its historical roots emerge, to see the present practices saturated with the voices of the people of the past—not only the great hymnists, composers, and performers, but the people who had stood in each pew and choir bench, singing their faith just two generations ago. Rather than stressing the view that a new organist or choir director *brought something* new to a congregation, I began to emphasize that they *joined something* that had a life prior to their coming. The particular musical practices of a congregation belonged not only to the director of music but to all the people in that church. Their *joint* responsibility was to nourish these practices and pass them on to the next generation, refurbished and changed to include the voices of the present faithful.

This shifted view of the vocation has several things to recommend it.

First, it works against its trivialization by recognizing that what musicians do in the church is to teach faith. Singing hymns, responses, choruses, parts of the communion rite, etc. teaches people their faith. Through the growth and renewal of musical practices, many *religious* traditions are maintained by congregations, kept alive, and passed down from generation to generation. Although the arts may appear to be peripheral in most parts of our society, in the church they are a central ingredient in its teaching ministry and in worship. The centrality of music to faith should convince people that support for the music program and its musicians is an important responsibility of each congregation. They should seek out good musicians and support their life among them with resources of "time and treasure." They should acknowledge that they, too, are church musicians and regain their treasured congregational singing traditions.

Second, this view breaks down the isolation from which many church musicians suffer, by spreading out the responsibility for the music in worship to include the community whose musical tradition it really is. It breaks it down by encouraging people to see themselves as joining a group of practicing musicians and by discouraging them to think of themselves as a musical version of the "Lone Ranger." This shared responsibility, however, must be honored by the congregation. Do they understand the importance of what they do? Do they recognize what it takes to maintain a musical tradition—the discipline required?

Third, this view honors the fact that musical practices have pasts. In the rush to become enticing to the "Unchurched," present-day congregations are giving up the musical traditions long associated with their worship life, in favor of "a new song," as if the hymns and anthems of the past had no value to them. The power of the present—the "moment" —obscures the fact that this current congregation did not invent their music program but received it as a gift from their forbears, who include not only their parents and grandparents, but the saints of the church as well. A congregation's identity is carried in these musical traditions; losing contact with them creates a shadowy identity in which the present obliterates that which gave it its form.

"Where to from here?"

Music in Your Church

The traditional disciplines of church music—playing the organ or piano, conducting choirs, choosing music—are grounded in the lived religion of a community, past, present and future. Aids to the discovery of this life of faith and the music that carries it are found in the appendix to the book and in a separately published research supplement. These formed the basis for the project. The *questionnaire* [Appendix A] is designed in four parts: the first to discover why people come to church, how they understand the church as a religious institution, its mission, and its activities. The second section asks pertinent questions about music. The third asks questions about faith and about worship. The fourth deals with demographic information. The *participant/observer forms* [published separately] were used by teams of researchers who visited the eight case-study churches on an "ordinary" Sunday. These gave us a detailed description of worship in a congregation from the viewpoint of three specialists—a musician, a scholar in worship, and a sociologist. The *interviews* [published separately] work to uncover both the idealized view of the church, its worship and its music, and the actual practice of these things in a local congregation. Also in the *recall schedules* there is no separate form for this; we asked a series of questions about worship immediately after church on a Sunday. We asked selected lay people to take the worship bulletin and, item by item, relate what they were doing or thinking about at that time. This latter interview structure was open-ended. The interviewee was encouraged to elaborate on their experiences in church, thereby allowing us to get a flavor of the congregation. These data were joined with a *survey* [Appendix B] containing a brief history of the congregation, written by the pastor or head of the worship committee.

Any of these methods can be used by a congregation to help discover the faith of the people and how music expresses it. This kind of research gives people an opportunity to discuss those things that are of the greatest importance to them. Aside from gleaning important information, people have a wonderful time undertaking the study. It can change their lives. In singing, we are giving voice to faith; to most people it is a powerful thing to do. The act of giving one's deepest being—that being "hid in Christ"—sensuous form has the capacity to transform one's life. In it, people join God's act in creating a world in which God and the faithful are one. In it, we join God in the ongoing act of incarnation.

The Questionnaire for the Music in Churches Project

This questionnaire is an adaptation of the one used in the Notre Dame study of American Catholic parishes. It is comprehensive in scope and designed to elicit information about the musical life of a congregation and its relationship to the faith of the people who gather on Sunday. It is long and complex, and, therefore, takes a significant block of time to complete. In the project, it was handed out after worship one Sunday morning together with a stamped, return envelope. Approximately half of them were returned.

Any or all of this questionnaire may be used by interested congregations. We used a numerical coding system to insure that people's views would remain confidential. The results may be tabulated by hand or by the various computer programs designed for such data.

The questionnaire elicited a broad overview of the congregation's musical and religious identity. Its purpose was to describe the congregation rather than to evaluate the music program in the churches. The interviews deepened and made explicit the general trends seen in the results of the questionnaire. Putting the two types of data together—the quantitative information from the questionnaire and the qualitative information from the interviews—was a highly effective way to study the complex and elusive questions of the project.

Part I

The questions in this section are addressed to you as a member of a church community. They include questions about why you come to church, why you stay, and what you do here. Your answers help us to understand the community that makes music in worship on Sunday.

(1) Put the date and time of the service of worship in which you received this questionnaire:

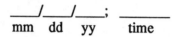

```
____/____/____;  _____
 mm   dd   yy      time
```

(2) In what year did you start attending this church?   19____

(3) What drew you to begin attending this particular church? *(Circle one.)*

01 Neighborhood location
02 It is the only church of this denomination in this town
03 The preaching
04 The music program
05 Fellowship
06 Youth program
07 The education program
08 The building
09 It's my family's church
10 Other: _____

(4) With so many competing demands placed on our time, it's often difficult to get involved in many activities, committees, auxiliaries, or ministries in a church. For what types of such activities have you been able to find time? *(Circle one.)*

1.   I haven't been able to participate in any church activities, committees, auxiliaries, etc. yet.

2A. I have been able to participate in some activities.
(List all activities in the space under "Activities" below.)

B. On the average, about how many hours per month do you
participate in each? *(Use the space in the B column below.)*

*List all activities in Column A. Please give a clear description of the
activity if there isn't a recognizable name or title for it. List the approxi-
mate hours per month you spend on the activity in Column B.*

Activities	Hrs/mo

(5) Think of five persons who are your closest friends. (Do not include
relatives.) How many of these friends are also members of your
church? *(Circle one.)*

0 1 2 3 4 5

(6) In general, how well does this parish meet:
(Circle one number beside each statement.)

	Completely	Very well	Not very well	Not at all
Your spiritual needs	1	2	3	4
Your social needs	1	2	3	4

(7) People go to church for different reasons. From the list below, please circle *only the most important* reason you attend worship at your church. *(Circle one.)*

    1. Mainly, it's a habit.
    2. I want to please or satisfy someone close to me (e.g., spouse or parent).
    3. I want to set an example for my children.
    4. I enjoy being with other persons in our church.
    5. I enjoy taking part in the service itself.
    6. I enjoy the feeling of meditating and communicating with God.
    7. I feel a need to hear God's word.
    8. I feel a need to receive the sacrament of Holy Communion.
    9. Other *(Indicate reason in the space.)*

_____

(8) In general, how attached to this particular church do you feel? *(Circle one.)*

    1. Not attached at all
    2. Somewhat attached
    3. Very attached

(9) Sometimes you hear people express satisfaction or dissatisfaction with the way worship is conducted in their local church. How would you rate the quality of public worship at your church? *(Circle one for each letter.)*

Key: 1 = Generally unsatisfactory
          2 = Could be improved
          3 = Generally satisfactory

1. Music	1	2	3
2. Scripture readings	1	2	3
3. Sermon	1	2	3
4. Congrgational singing	1	2	3
5. Prayers	1	2	3
6. Ritual	1	2	3

(10) In your own words, what do you think the main purpose of a local church is supposed to be?

(11) The following statements reflect various activities of the church. For each item would you indicate whether this activity is very important, somewhat important, not very important, or contradic tory to your understanding of the church's mission in today's world.

Key: 1 = CT = Contradictory to
2 = NI = Not very important
3 = SI = Somewhat important
4 = VI = Very important

How important is . . .

		CT	NI	SI	VI
1.	Providing adult education re-sources that bring laity face to face with urban and rural problems, ra-cial discrimination, world poverty and hunger, and other social issues.				
2.	Establishing new churches.	1	2	3	4
3.	Helping church members resist the temptation to experiment with new lifestyles.	1	2	3	4
4.	Actively reaching out to members of other religious groups with an invitation to find true salvation.	1	2	3	4
5.	Encouraging pastors of local churches to speak out in public on social, political, and economic is-sues that confront American society today.	1	2	3	4
6.	Opening members' hearts and minds to the spiritual gifts of miracles and healing, and to the baptism of the Holy Spirit.	1	2	3	4

7. Encouraging church members to   1   2   3   4
   reach their own decisions on issues
   of faith and morals even if this diminishes the church's ability to speak
   with a single voice on these issues.

8. Promoting social justice in North   1   2   3   4
   America and throughout the world
   by the use of organized, collective
   action.

9. Reminding Christians of their duty   1   2   3   4
   to uphold and defend their country
   and the values it stands for.

10. Protecting church members from   1   2   3   4
    the false teachings of other reli-
    gious groups.

11. Encouraging church members to   1   2   3   4
    adhere faithfully to civil laws, even
    when they disagree with them.

12. Listening carefully to what the   1   2   3   4
    world is saying in order to under-
    stand what the church's ministry
    should be about.

13. Encouraging church members to   1   2   3   4
    make explicit declarations of their
    personal faith to friends, neighbors
    and co-workers.

14. Making the church a place where   1   2   3   4
    people of all classes and races are
    included.

15. Encouraging and inspiring church   1   2   3   4
    members, as individuals, to become
    involved in social and political issues.

16. Finding ways to involve women   1   2   3   4
    and minority persons in decision-
    making roles within the church.

17. Supporting evangelical missions   1   2   3   4
    overseas to convert the world to
    Christ.

18. Providing relief and physical sup-   1   2   3   4
    port to people and groups in need
    in this country and around the
    world.

19. Maintaining an appropriate dis-   1   2   3   4
    tance between the churches and
    governmental affairs.

20. Preparing church members for a   1   2   3   4
    world to come in which the cares
    of this world are absent.

21. Encouraging members to develop   1   2   3   4
    their spiritual life through prayer
    and Bible study.

(12) Which of the following best describes why you continue to attend
     this church? *(Circle only one response.)*

   01 It's my church; I live in this neighborhood.
   02 Quality of friendliness and/or concern among church members.
   03 The opportunities for becoming a lay leader in the congrega-
      tion.
   04 The atmosphere of the church building itself.
   05 The quality of pastoral care and concern provided by the staff
      and laity.
   06 The quality of the preaching.
   07 The music program.
   08 The opportunity for community service.
   09 The style of worship that is typical of the church.
   10 The fact that many of my friends and/or relatives belong to this
      church.
   11 The quality of religious education.
   12 The youth ministry.
   13 Other reasons *(Please write reasons in this space.)*

   _____

   _____

(13) How upsetting would it be for you if you had to move and were forced to leave this particular church? *(Circle one.)*

  1. Very upsetting
  2. Mildly upsetting
  3. Not very upsetting
  4. Not upsetting at all

(14) Next is a question about your church as a community. Some churches are tightly-knit, and people feel close to one another; others are less tightly-knit, less intimately bound to one another. On a scale of 1 to 5, 5 being the most closely knit, where would you put your church? *(Put an "X" at the appropriate place on the line.)*

1   2   3   4   5
_____

(15) How would you assess the importance of worship in this church to your ongoing faith? *(Circle only one.)*

  1. Very important
  2. Important
  3. Not very important
  4. Of no importance

Part II

This next set of questions concerns your musical interests and talents. It helps us gain information about a congregation's view of music in worship and their participation in it.

(16) Do you consider yourself a musician?

    1. Yes   2. No

(17) Circle the church musical organizations or activities in which you have participated in the last five years.

    1. Adult choir
    2. Junior choir
    3. Youth choir
    4. Handbells
    5. Instrumental groups
    6. Other: _____

(18) Do you read music?

    1. Yes   2. No

(19) Do you play a musical instrument?

    1 . Yes   2. No

    If yes, what kind? _____

(20) Do you participate in musical organizations in the outside community (e.g., choral societies, instrumental ensembles, barber shop quartets, jazz bands.)

    1. Yes   2. No

    If yes, what kind? _____

(21) In the last six months have you participated in formal or informal group singing anywhere else but in church?

   1. Yes   2. No

   If yes, please list what kind? _____

(22) How often do you listen to music on the radio?

   Number of hours a week: _____
   Principal radio stations: _____

(23) How often do you attend public concerts?

   1. Once a month
   2. Twice a month
   3. Less frequently than once a month
   4. More frequently than twice a month

(24) List the last public concert you attended: _____

(25) The world is filled with all kinds of music. *Arrange the following list of "musics" in order of your preference by numbering them 1 - 10.*

   ___ 01 Folk music
   ___ 02 Rock 'n' roll
   ___ 03 Jazz and the blues
   ___ 04 Classical/symphonic
   ___ 05 Opera
   ___ 06 Musical comedies
   ___ 07 Sacred music
   ___ 08 Gospel music (anthems, oratorios, organ music, etc.)
   ___ 09 Chamber music
   ___ 10 Other: _____

(26) How important to you is the music program in this church? *(Circle one.)*

    1. Very important
    2. Important
    3. Not important
    4. There is no program, and I do not care to have one started.
    5. There is no program, and I wish there were one.

(27) How would you rate the music program in this church? *(Circle one.)*

    1. Excellent
    2. Good
    3. Needs improvement
    4. Drastic change is called for

(28) If you could make *one* change in the present music program to make it more effective, what would it be?

(29) Would you advocate *increasing* the resources for music in this church?

    1. Yes   2. No

(30) What part of the music in worship is the most meaningful to you? *(Indicate your preferences in order by numbering three of the following list 1st, 2nd, 3rd.)*

    ___ 1. Hymns
    ___ 2. Anthems by the choir and/or soloists
    ___ 3. Settings of the psalms
    ___ 4. Organ prelude
    ___ 5. Organ postlude
    ___ 6. Chanting the liturgy and/or other liturgical responses
    ___ 7. Instrumental music
    ___ 8. Other: _____

(31) How would you rank yourself as a singer? *(Circle one.)*

1. I don't like to sing.
2. I like to sing but don't do it well
3. I like to sing and do it well.
4. I do not like to sing but enjoy standing and listening to others.

(32) Most services of worship include hymn singing. *Please choose one* of the following statements which best describes your attitude toward the use of hymns in worship.

1. Hymn singing is essential to worship. (I.e., if there is no hymn singing, there is no worship.)
2. Hymn singing adds an important ingredient to worship but is not essential to it.
3. Hymn singing is an enjoyable aspect of worship but is neither essential or important.
4. Hymn singing is an insignificant aspect of worship.

(33) Which of the following statements comes the closest to your view of the *use of music* in worship? *(Circle one.)*

1. Hymn singing is essential to worship. (I.e., if there is no hymn singing, there is no worship.)
2. Hymn singing adds an important ingredient to worship but is not essential to it.
3. Hymn singing is an enjoyable aspect of worship but is neither essential or important.
4. Hymn singing is an insignificant aspect of worship.

(34) Which of the following statements comes the closest to your view of *the kind of music* to be used in worship? *(Circle one.)*

1. All styles of music are appropriate to worship.
2. Any music is appropriate as long as it is sung or played with sincerity.
3. Any kind of music is appropriate as long as I find it enjoyable.

4. Since music in worship is an offering to God, only the best is appropriate.
5. Any kind of music is appropriate as long as the congregation can use it to praise God.
6. Other: _____

(35) Below are frequently voiced statements about church music programs. What is *your* view of these opinions? *(Circle one number for each statement.)*

	Strongly Agree	Mildy Agree	Mildly Disagree	Strongly Disagree
1. The guitar doesn't belong in the church.	1	2	3	4
2. The music program should be used to attract people to worship on Sunday.	1	2	3	4
3. The choir should be all volunteers.	1	2	3	4
4. The purpose of hymn singing is to unite a congregation in feeling and purpose.	1	2	3	4
5. A single theme or idea based on Scripture should unite all the music in worship.	1	2	3	4
6. The minister should choose the hymns.	1	2	3	4
7. New music disrupts worship.	1	2	3	4
8. A committee consisting of staff and lay leaders should have control over the music program in the church.	1	2	3	4

	Strongly Agree	Mildy Agree	Mildly Dis-agree	Strong-ly Dis-agree
9. You can tell a good music program by the style of music used.	1	2	3	4
10. The old hymns are the best.	1	2	3	4
11. The music program should serve the mission (outreach) of the church.	1	2	3	4
12. The purpose of hymn singing is to deepen my relationship with God.	1	2	3	4
13. The director of music should choose the hymns.	1	2	3	4

(36) Hymns often teach us very powerful lessons about God and God's relationship to us. Think of your favorite hymn. *(If you have several, please choose the one that first came to mind.)*

1. What is your favorite hymn?

   _____

2. What is the basic image of God in it?

   _____

3. What is the view of the human—the singer(s)—in it?

   _____

4. What is the relationship between God and humanity in it?

   _____

5. Why is this hymn your favorite?

   _____

Part III

Here the questions are addressed to you as a person of faith. They provide an opportunity for you to describe what your religious faith really means to you.

(37) How often do you go to each of the following?
(Circle only one number beside each)

1. Sunday services	1	2	3	4	5	6	7	8
2. Sunday school	1	2	3	4	5	6	7	8
3. Mid-week services	1	2	3	4	5	6	7	8
4. Prayer meetings	1	2	3	4	5	6	7	8
5. Holy Communion	1	2	3	4	5	6	7	8

6. Other *(please list)* _____

1	2	3	4	5	6	7	8

(38) How often do you do the following?
(Circle one number for each.)

1. Read or study the Bible on your own	1	2	3	4	5	6	7	8
2. Read or study the Bible with friends or as part of a group	1	2	3	4	5	6	7	8
3. Say Grace before meals	1	2	3	4	5	6	7	8
4. Share your religious beliefs with others who have *similar* beliefs	1	2	3	4	5	6	7	8
5. Share your religious beliefs with those who have *different* beliefs	1	2	3	4	5	6	7	8

6. Listen to a religious 1   2   3   4   5   6   7   8
program on radio
(Specify which pro-
grams.)

7. Watch a religious pro- 1   2   3   4   5   6   7   8
gram on TV
(Specify which pro-
grams)

8. Pray with members of 1   2   3   4   5   6   7   8
family or friends other
than Grace

9. Pray privately   1   2   3   4   5   6   7   8

10. Go on other retreats or 1   2   3   4   5   6   7   8
other religious week-
ends or gatherings

(39) Below is a list of images that could be used to describe God.
Indicate how accurate you feel each is as a description of God

1. Judge   1   2   3   4   5

2. Protector   1   2   3   4   5

3. Redeemer   1   2   3   4   5

4. Lover   1   2   3   4   5

5. Master   1   2   3   4   5

6. Mother   1   2   3   4   5

7. Creator   1   2   3   4   5

8. Father   1   2   3   4   5

9. Friend   1   2   3   4   5

(40) As you read each of the following phrases, indicate how true it is for you. *(Circle only one number beside each statement or phrase.)*

1.	Faithful	1	2	3	4	5
2.	Dependable	1	2	3	4	5
3.	Forgiving	1	2	3	4	5
4.	Mysterious	1	2	3	4	5
5.	More present in relationships with others than in an individual's life	1	2	3	4	5
6.	Distant	1	2	3	4	5
7.	Permissive	1	2	3	4	5
8.	A creative force in history	1	2	3	4	5
9.	Aware of everything I think!	1	2	3	4	5
10.	Close	1	2	3	4	5
11.	Vindictive	1	2	3	4	5
12.	My constant companion	1	2	3	4	5
13.	Strict	1	2	3	4	5
14.	Clearly knowable	1	2	3	4	5
15.	In my life more as a symbol or an idea than as a real presence I can feel	1	2	3	4	5
16.	All-powerful	1	2	3	4	5
17.	Awesome	1	2	3	4	5

18. Fascinating	1	2	3	4	5
19. Judgmental	1	2	3	4	5
20. Indifferent	1	2	3	4	5

(41) Which one of these six pictures best symbolizes your own idea of God's relationship to the world? *(Circle one.)*

1. God and the world are one.

2. The world is part of God, but God is greater and larger than the world.

3. Human beings are part of God.

4. God sets the world in motion but does not play an active role in the world.

5. God transcends the world, entering the world infrequently.

6. God transcends the world, but is actively involved in the world.

(42) The nature of God has often been a matter of dispute in the history
of the church. Each of us carries around our own picture of the
interrelationship of God, Jesus Christ, and ourselves. Which of the
following pictures comes closest to the way you see it?
(Please circle only one.)

1. God has sent the Son,
    Jesus, to save us and
    since God has com-
    pleted that, each of us
    individually can ap-
    proach God directly.

2. God has sent the Son,
    Jesus, to save us and
    since God has done that
    and continues to do it,
    us each of us individu-
    ally can approach God
    through Jesus.

3. God has sent the Son,
    Jesus, who continues to
    live in the church. As a
    result, the church
    teaches and sanctifies
    us for God.

4. Since the Church is Christ's
    body and since we, its mem-
    bers, are the church, together
    we approach God.

5. Jesus was a great man but not
    really god. *Jesus showed how
    to live our lives.*

6. Do you have some other
    picture? *(Please describe and
    illustrate.)*

    _____

    _____

    _____

(43)   Below are six drawings of people at worship. *Circle the one that most clearly captures your view of worship at its best. There is a space included for you to add one of your own if the others are inadequate.*

(44) The following questions deal with your feelings of "closeness" to God in different situations. *(Please circle only one number for each statement. Omit those which are not applicable to your experience.)*

Key: 1 = Not close at all   3 = Somewhat close   5 = Very close

1. Reading the Bible	1	2	3	4	5
2. Gathering with members of the congregation	1	2	3	4	5
3. Attending worship	1	2	3	4	5
4. Singing in church	1	2	3	4	5
5. Receiving Holy Communion	1	2	3	4	5
6. Praying privately	1	2	3	4	5
7. Helping individuals in need	1	2	3	4	5
8. Working for the church	1	2	3	4	5
9. Working for justice and peace	1	2	3	4	5
10. Walking by the sea or hiking in the mountains	1	2	3	4	5
11. Being with the person I love	1	2	3	4	5
12. Going on retreats	1	2	3	4	5
13. Meeting with a small church group for prayer and support	1	2	3	4	5
14. Obeying the ten commandments	1	2	3	4	5

(45) How often in your life *have you had an experience* where you felt
     as though you were very close to a powerful, spiritual force that
     seemed to lift you out of yourself? *(Circle one.)*

     1. Never in my life *(Skip the next question.)*
     2. Once or twice
     3. Several times
     4. Often

(46) When you have or had these religious experiences, what happened?
     (e.g., When did it happen? How did it happen? How did you feel?
     Why did you think it was a spiritual force? *(Please describe. Use
     the reverse of this page if necessary.)*

Part IV

It is important for us to know not only why you come *to sing* on Sunday morning but also who you are. *Please answer the following general questions about yourself.*

(47) Sex   1. Male ____   2. Female ____

(48) What is your present marital status?

1. Never married
2. Married and living with spouse
3. Separated
4. Divorced and now single
5. Divorced and now remarried
6. Widow or widower

(49) Do you have any children? If so, how many and what are their ages?

1. I have no children.
2. I have one child.
3. I have_____children.
    (a) List the ages of the youngest and the oldest below.
        Youngest: ___   Oldest: ___

(50) Besides being an American, what is your main nationality back ground? *(Circle those that apply.)*

01 American (no other nationality)
02 English
03 Scot, Welsh
04 Afro-American
05 French-speaking Canadian
06 French

07 Eastern European
08 Italian
09 Portuguese
10 Asian (Korean, Chinese, Japanese, Vietnamese, etc.)
11 Middle Eastern (Lebanese, Syrian, Egyptian, etc.)
12 Amer-Indian
13 German
14 Hispanic
15 English-speaking Canadian
16 Scandinavian
17 Irish
18 West Indian
19 Other: _____

(51) Please indicate the highest level of education you have completed.
    (Circle only one.)

    1. 8th grade or less
    2. Some high school
    3. High school graduate
    4. Some college
    5. Technical school or two year (junior college) degree
    6. Completed college
    7. Some graduate work
    8. Graduate or professional degree (M.A., PH.D., M.D. etc.)

(52) Age (in years): _____

(53) Which of the following labels best describes your political position?
    (Circle only one.)

    1. Very liberal
    2. Liberal
    3. Moderate
    4. Conservative
    5. Very conservative
    6. Other *(please describe)*: _____

(54) *List your occupation. Please try to be as clear and specific as possible.* For example if you work as a lathe operator in a factory you should enter "lathe operator" and not skilled tradesman, blue-collar w*orker, etc. I*f you are presently retired, indicate "retired" and list your principal former occupation.

(55) How many years have you lived in your current residence?
_____ years

(56) How far is your present home from the church you attend? *(Circle one.)*

1. Less than 1 mile   4. 3 - 5 miles
2. 1 - 2 miles   5. 5 - 10 miles
3. 2 - 3 miles   6. More than 10 miles

(57) In which of the categories listed below would you put your total family income (from all sources, before taxes) for last year? *(Circle one.)*

1. Under $10,000   6. 40,000 - 44,999
2. Between 10,000 - 19,999 7. 45,000 - 49,999
3. 20,000 - 29,999   8. 50,000 - 59,999
4. 30,000 - 34,999   9. 60,000 and over
5. 35,000 - 39,999

(58) *We are interested in your denominational background.* In column
A, circle the number for the present denominational background. In
column B. Circle the number for the denomination in which you
were raised. In column C. Circle the number(s), if any, for any other
denomination to which you have belonged;

	A	B	C
Episcopal	01	01	01
United Methodist	02	02	02
Baptist	03	03	03
Roman Catholic	04	04	04
UCC/Congregational	05	05	05
Lutheran	06	06	06
Pentecostal	07	07	07
Presbyterian	08	08	08
Orthodox	09	09	09
Unitarian/Universalist	10	10	10
None	11	11	11
Other	12	12	12

You have reached the end of the questionnaire. Thank you for your time
and thoughtful consideration of the questions. You have made a valuable
contribution to this study.

Interview Protocols for the Music in Churches Project

These interviews were given by members of the research team in each of the eight case-study churches. Their format was consistently followed so that information could be compared among the interviewees and the eight congregations. The comparison between what "should be" and "what was" elicited very valuable information about each of these churches from those interviewed. We asked both the musician and the pastor for suggestions of people to interview. We also went up to people randomly during visits to choir rehearsals and other church events and asked to interview them. Again, all the information gathered was confidential, thus assuring that if conflicts existed in the congregation, people's particular viewpoints were not broadcast with their names attached. In subsequent publications, like this one, all names of the churches, their locations, and the people in them are changed.

Approximately ten interviews were given in each of the case-study churches. They garnered invaluable information about worship and music in these congregations. Their purpose was both descriptive and evaluative. For the most part, people spoke readily of their religious experience and the centrality of music to it. From them we learned about the religious identity of the congregation through the eyes of its members. We also had a firsthand look at the music program over a long period of time. These interviews can be given by members of one's congregation. We would suggest that the pastor and musician not be among the interviewers, however. Perhaps a member of the worship committee or session or vestry could be enlisted to do them.

The other important source of information about the worship and music of the case-study churches was the *Recall Schedule* done immediately after worship on the Sunday morning the team showed up in church. (This interview format was derived from the Georgetown study of the liturgy.) The team sat down with a lay person and the bulletin for that Sunday in hand, went through it, asking him or her what they were thinking or feeling at that particular moment. This interview structure was much more open-ended than the other, although the researcher was bound to complete the bulletin. The purpose of this interview was to elicit stories and other descriptions of the way the interviewee connected his or her faith life with facets of Sunday worship.

All of these interviews were recorded and then transcribed.

Interviews with Pastor or Priest

Biographical information: training, how long in church, position, etc.

1. Your view of the church

    a. Give me three adjectives or phrases that describe what a church ought to be.
    b. Enlarge on the one that is the most important to you at this time in your ministry.
    c. Give me three adjectives that describe this church.
    d. Give an image or phrase that the people of the town would use to describe this church. Is it an accurate view?

2. Your concept of the ministry

    a. Give me three adjectives that would describe what ministry (in general, not necessarily ordained) should be.
    b. Enlarge on the one that is the most important to you at this time.
    c. Give three adjectives that describe *your* ministry in this church.

3. Your view of worship

    a. Give me three adjectives that would describe the role of worship in a community of faith.
    b. Enlarge on the one that is most important to you at this time.
    c. Give me three adjectives that would describe worship here.
    d. Where does worship stand in importance among all activities in the congregation's life?
    e. Could you hazard a guess why it appears there?
    f. Do you think your church's worship has vitality? On what basis do you make this judgment?
    g. How does planning for worship take place in this congregation?

4. Your view of music

    a. Give me three phrases to describe how music should function in worship.
    b. Give me three adjectives that would describe how music does function in this church.
    c. What is the congregational singing like?
    d. What is the role of the choir in worship?
    e. What is the role of organ/piano in worship?

Is there anything you would like to enlarge on from the issues we have discussed in the interview?

Interviews with Musician/Head of Music Committee

Biographical information: training, how long in church, position, etc.

1. Your view of the church

   a. Give me three adjectives or phrases that describe what a church ought to be.
   b. Enlarge on the one that is the most important to you at this time.
   c. Give me three adjectives that would describe this church.

2. Your concept of ministry

   a. Do you consider what you (the church musician) do a form of ministry? Why or why not?

3. Your view of worship

   a. Give me three phrases that would describe the role of worship in a community of faith.
   b. Enlarge on the one that is most important to you at this time.
   c. Give me three phrases that would describe worship here.
   d. Do you think your church's worship has vitality? On what basis do you make this judgment?
   g. How does planning for worship take place?

4. Your view of music

   a. Give me three phrases that would describe how music should function in worship.
   b. Please enlarge on the one that you think is the most important.
   c. Give me three phrases that would describe the music program in this church.

For the musician only:

    d. What is budget?
    e. How does music planning take place?
    f. What is the congregational singing like?
    g. What is the role of the choir, the organ in worship?
    h. How do you tell good music from bad?
    i. How do you know when you're successful?
    j. Why do you do what you do?
    k. What is the musical life of the congregation like outside the church?

l. Who chooses the hymns?

Is there anything you would like to enlarge on from the issues we have discussed in the interview?

Interviews with Lay People

Biographical information: connection with church, position, activities, etc.

1. Your view of the church

   a. Give me three adjectives or phrases that describe what a church ought to be.
   b. Enlarge on the one that you think the most important at this point in your life.
   c. Give me three adjectives or phrases that describe this church.
   d. Give an image or phrase that the people of the town would use to describe this church. Is this an accurate view?

2. Your concept of ministry

   a. Would you say that what your church musician does is a form of ministry. Why or why not?

3. Your view of worship

   a. Give me three adjectives or phrases that would describe the role of worship in a community of faith.
   b. Enlarge on the most important of those.
   c. Give me three adjectives that would describe worship in this church.
   d. When you think of all the things that your church community does, where would worship stand in importance?
   e. Could you hazard a guess why it appears there?
   f. Do you think your church's worship has vitality? On what basis do you make this judgment?

4. Your view of music in worship

    a. Give me three phrases that would describe how music should
        function in worship.
    b. Enlarge on the most important of those.
    c. Give me three adjectives that would describe the music program
        of this church.
    d. What is you view of the role of the choir in worship?
    e. What is your view of the role of the organ in worship?
    f. Obviously, music in worship is very important to me. . . . Why is
        it important to you personally?
    g. If you could be "church musician" for a week, what would you
        do?
    h. How would you rate the congregational singing? Why?

Is there anything you would like to enlarge on from the issues we have
discussed in the interviews?

Anything to add?

SELECTED BIBLIOGRAPHY

Music in Churches

Allen, Pamela. "Singing a faithful song: Brian Wren's hymns of justice," *Christian Century*, July,1985.

Benson, Louis. *The English Hymn*. Philadelphia: Doran, 1915.

Blume, Friedrich. *Protestant Church Music*. New York: W. W. Norton, 1974.

Boyer, Horace Clarence. An analysis of Black church music with examples drawn from services in Rochester, New York. Unpub. Ph.D. diss., Eastman School of Music, 1973.

Brown, E. Kent. Historical perspectives on Methodist worship," *Religion in Life*, 1970 (39).

Cameron, Kenneth Walter, ed. *Early Anglican Church Music in America*. Hartford: Transcendental Books, 1983. 2 vols.

Clark, Keith. *A Selective Bibliography for the Study of Hymns*. Wittenburg, 1980.

Clark, Linda. "A view from the pew," *The Hymn*, January, 1992.

———— "In Christ there is no East or West," in *Language about God in Liturgy and Scripture*. Philadelphia: Geneva, 1980.

———— "Hymn-singing: aesthetic forms as carriers of religious tradition." Carl Dudley et al. *Carriers of Faith*. Louisville: Westminster/John Knox Press, 1991.

———— *Music in Churches Project Reports*. Boston University Occasional Papers, 1990-1992.

Cobb, Buell. *The Sacred Harp*. Athens, GA: University of Georgia Press, 1978.

Cohen, Charles L. *God's Caress: The Psychology of Puritan Religious Experience*. New York: Oxford University Press, 1986.

Cone, James. *Spirituals and the Blues*. New York: Seabury Press, 1972.

Cook, Harold. *Shaker Music*. Lewisburg: Bucknell Press, 1973.

Crawford, Richard, ed. *The Core Repertory of Early American Psalmody*. Recent researches in American music, vols. XI and XII; Madison: A-R editions, 1984.

Davis, Arthur. *Isaac Watts*. New York: Dryden Press, 1943.

Dearnley, Christopher. *English Church Music: 1650-1750*. London: Barrie and Jenkins, 1970.

Diehl, Katherine. *Hymns and Tunes—an Index*. New York: Scarecrow, 1966.

Epstein, Dena. "African music in British and French America," *MQ* 1973 (59).

——— *Sinful Tunes and Spirituals*. Urbana: University of Illinois, 1977.

Filbert, Mark. "Hymnody in a local congregation," *Reform Liturgy and Music*, 1982 (33).

Garside, Charles. "Some attitudes of the major reformers toward the role of music in the liturgy," *McCormick Quarterly*, 1967 (21).

——— "Calvin's preface to the Psalter," *Musical Quarterly*, 1951 (37).

Geertz, Clifford. "Art as a cultural system," *ML NOTES*, 1976 (91).

——— "Ethos, world view, and the analysis of sacred symbols," in *The Interpretation of Symbols*. New York: Basic books, 1973.

Hanson, Paul D. *The People Called: the Growth of Community in the Bible*. San Francisco: Harper and Row, 1986.

Hayburn, Robert. *Papal Legislation on Sacred Music*. Collegeville: Liturgical Press, 1979.

Heard, Priscilla. *American Music 1698-1800, an Annotated Bibliography*. Waco: Baylor University, 1975.

Heisey, Terry. "Singet Hallelujah! Music in the Evangelical Association, 1800-1894," *Methodist History*, 1990 (28).

Hitchcock, H. Wiley. *Music in the United States: a Historical Introduction*. 2nd ed. Englewood Cliffs: Prentice-Hall, 1974.

Hood, George. *A History of Music in New England*. Boston: Wilkins, Carter, 1846.

Hoon, Paul. *The Integrity of Worship*. Nashville: Abingdon, 1971.

Julian, John. *A Dictionary of Hymnology*. Second revised edition with new supplement. New York: Dover, 1957.

Leaver, Robin. *The Liturgy and Music*. Bramcote: Grove Books, 1976.

LeHuray, Peter. *Music and the Reformation in England, 1549-1660*. New York: Oxford, 1967.

Lems-Dworkin, Carol, ed. World music center: *African and New World Black Music Bibliography*. Evanston: Northwestern University Press, program of African studies, n.d.

Manning, Bernard. *The Hymns of Watts and Wesley*. London, Epworth: 1942.

Mapson, J. Wendell, Jr. *The Ministry of Music in the Black Church*. Valley Forge: Judson Press, 1984.

McDormand, Thomas and Frederic Crossman, eds. *Judson Concordance to Hymns*. Valley Forge: Judson Press, 1965.

Meland, Bernard E. "Myth as a mode of awareness and intelligibility" *American Journal of Theology and Philosophy*, 1987 (8).

Mitchell, Robert. *Ministry and Music*. Philadelphia: Westminster Press, 1978.

Nichols, Kathryn. "Charles Wesley's Eucharistic hymns: their relationship to the Book of Common Prayer," *The Hymn* 1988 (39).

Procter-Smith, Marjorie. *In Her Own Rite*. Nashville: Abingdon, 1990.

Routley, Eric. *Church Music and the Christian Faith*. Carol Stream, Illinois: Agape Press, 1978.

——— *Divine Formula*. Princeton: Prestige, 1986.

——— *The Music of Christian Hymns*. Chicago: GIA, 1981.

Schaller, Joseph J. "Performative language theory: an exercise in the analysis of ritual," *Worship*, 1988 (62).

Seubert, Xavier John. "Weaving a pattern of access: the essence of ritual," *Worship*, 1989 (63).

Sizer, Sandra. *Gospel Hymns*. Philadelphia: Temple, 1978.

Southern, Eileen. *The Music of Black Americans*. New York: W. W. Norton, 1971.

Stevenson, Robert. "The Afro-American musical legacy to 1800." *MQ* 1968, (54).

Senn, Frank. "The dialogue between liturgy and music," *The Hymn*, 1987.

Sydnor, James. *Hymns and their uses*. Carol Stream: Agape Press, 1982.

Taylor, John E. "Somethin' on my mind: a cultural and historical interpretation of Spiritual texts," *Ethnomusicology*, 1975 (19), 387f.

This far by faith: American Black worship and its African roots. Washington, D. C.: National Office for Black Catholics and the Liturgical Conference, 1976.

Thompson, Bard. *Liturgies of the Western Church*. Cleveland: World Publishing, 1961.

Walker, Wyatt T. *Somebody's calling my name*. Valley Forge: Judson Press, 1979.

Waterman, Richard. "African influence on the music of the Americas," in *Acculturation in the Americas*. Sol Tax, ed., Chicago: University of Chicago Press, 1952.

Williams, Henry. "The hymnal of 1789: a Moravian landmark,"
  Moravian Music Journal, 1989 (34).

Williams-Jones, Pearl. "Afro-American gospel music: a crystallization
  of the Black aesthetic," *Ethnomusicology*, 1975 (19).

Wyeth, John. *Repository of Sacred Music, Part II*. New York: DaCapo
  Press, 1964 (orig. 1820).

The Alban Institute:
an invitation to membership

The Alban Institute, begun in 1979, believes that the congregation is essential to the task of equipping the people of God to minister in the church and the world. A multi-denominational membership organization, the Institute provides on-site training, educational programs, consulting, research, and publishing for hundreds of churches across the country.

The Alban Institute invites you to be a member of this partnership of laity, clergy, and executives—a partnership that brings together people who are raising important questions about congregational life and people who are trying new solutions, making new discoveries, finding a new way of getting clear about the task of ministry. The Institute exists to provide you with the kinds of information and resources you need to support your ministries.

Join us now and enjoy these benefits:

CONGREGATIONS: The Alban Journal, a highly respected journal published six times a year, to keep you up to date on current issues and trends.

Inside Information, Alban's quarterly newsletter, keeps you informed about research and other happenings around Alban. Available to members only.

Publications Discounts:

- 15% for Individual, Retired Clergy, and Seminarian Members
- 25% for Congregational Members
- 40% for Judicatory and Seminary Executive Members

Discounts on Training and Education Events

Write our Membership Department at the address below or call us at 1-800-486-1318 or 301-718-4407 for more information about how to join The Alban Institute's growing membership, particularly about Congregational Membership in which 12 designated persons receive all benefits of membership.

The Alban Institute, Inc.
Suite 433 North
4550 Montgomery Avenue
Bethesda, MD 20814-3341